ECOTOURISM

PRACTICES, BENEFITS
AND ENVIRONMENTAL IMPACTS

TOURISM AND HOSPITALITY DEVELOPMENT AND MANAGEMENT

ECOTOURISM

PRACTICES, BENEFITS AND ENVIRONMENTAL IMPACTS

SHANNON C. BROPHY
EDITOR

nova
publishers
New York

Library of Congress Cataloging-in-Publication Data
Ecotourism : practices, benefits and environmental impacts / editor: Shannon C. Brophy.
    pages cm. -- (Tourism and hospitality development and management)
  Includes index.
  ISBN 978-1-63482-027-1 (Hardcover)
  1. Ecotourism--Case studies. 2. Ecotourism--Environmental aspects--Case studies. I. Brophy, Shannon C., editor of compilation.
  G156.5.E26E356 2015
  338.4'791--dc23
                    2015001260

Published by Nova Science Publishers, Inc. † New York

CONTENTS

PREFACE

Tourism is defined as the set of activities of persons traveling to and staying for the sake of rest, leisure, culture, health, etc. in places that are outside their usual environment for a period not exceeding one year. Ecotourism or green tourism is a form of sustainable tourism, focused on the discovery and preservation of nature and ecosystems. Ecotourism's main objective is to discover and preserve different forms of natural resources such as fascinating landscapes, local flora and fauna, while respecting ecosystems, even helping to restore, in a voluntary approach. This book examines the practices of ecotourism as well as its benefits and impacts on the environment.

Chapter 1 – The main objective of this chapter is the analysis of tourism activities located in a given territory during their evolution and steady state life. Interventions to make tourism more sustainable are deeply analysed. Specific tools to improve sustainability of tourism are also discussed. Positive effects induced by regulated procedures such as SEA, EIA, EMAS, ISO14001, ECOLABEL, SWOT ANALYSIS are taken into consideration as well. Specific attention is devoted to the implementation of the EU Ecolabel in sustainable hotel management. Some other forms of environmental friendly sustainable tourism are also described. This chapter discusses positive results expected from various kinds of sustainable tourism in terms of reduction of resource consumption, pollutants and CO_2 emissions, solid waste management, preservation of biodiversity, etc. Much attention is given to indicators able to measure sustainability of tourism in a given territory, such as economic performance (Gross Domestic Product, GDP), quality of social life (Human Development Index, HDI), health conditions (Life Expectancy at birth), energy consumption, air and water quality, etc. More specific indicators directly connected with tourism are also investigated. Among them, one can mention specific indicators such as the amount of green area per person, number of hotels, number of rooms and residences for families, traffic congestion and noise, etc. Specific case studies are devoted to the life of tourism destinations according to the model developed by Butler. In the last part of the study the characterization of the area and the calculation of the specific indicators are described. The methodology is tested and applied to some specific areas with the aim at showing the dynamic nature of the destination life divided among different phases. For the selected destinations, adequate indicators are identified and quantified with the aim of improving the level of sustainability of different conditions.

Chapter 2 – Islands are among the most visited tourist destinations in the world. They are exposed to all kinds of risks with often inadequate resources and fragile ecosystems. The prospect of ecotourism development in tropical islands are enormous, since most islands host distinctive flora and fauna with some endemic species, colourful coral reefs and marine ecosystems, as well as unique environmental features and appealing land- and seascapes. Brunei Darussalam has 33 islands spread across its shores, which are largely uninhabited. Among them is Selirong Island, an island dominantly covered by mangrove forests, which has been developed as an ecotourism destination. This chapter begins with a historical overview of the development of Selirong Island as a forest production site and now as an ecotourism attraction, and later examines how interpretation can be used as a tool for the conservation and preservation of its rich biodiversity, as well as for the environmental education of tourists and visitors to the island.

Chapter 3 – The Campos Gerais National Park, situated in southern Brazil, was created in 2006 with the aim of conserving the last remaining ecosystems of native grasslands and Araucaria Forest; the phytogeographical area of Atlantic Forest biome. Campos Gerais National Park (CGNP) is one of 68 Brazilian national parks. It is managed by the Chico Mendes Institute for Biodiversity Conservation (ICMBio) as an IUCN (International Union for Conservation of Nature) Category II conservation unit. Although resource protection is a critical management focus at CGNP, public use activities are also very popular within the conservation area. Public use has the potential to generate significant negative impacts to the natural environment and the quality of the visitor's experience if not managed appropriately. Accordingly, this case study is an analysis of visitation activities and their impacts at Mariquinha Waterfall, one of the most important and most-visited attractions in Campos Gerais National Park (CGNP). Resource managers used the Visitor Impact Management (VIM) process in planning this study which focuses intensely on visitor experiences and the protection of natural and cultural resources. VIM is a visitor monitoring framework used as a guideline for collecting and organizing data, assisting with the management actions related to visitor impact, and serves to support the decisions made by managers. The results of this study showed distinct differences in seasonal visitation at places such as the Mariquinha Waterfall, while other tourist resources in the area receive lower use. Furthermore, managers identified a younger local audience that seeks contact with nature. Most importantly, the study considered both existing and potential tourism activities in the area, with the idea of providing the user a range of possible activities. In conclusion, our findings recommend that efforts should be invested to further study and develop tourism opportunities in natural areas in this park.

Chapter 4 – Colombia is considered one of the most biodiversity and cultural rich countries worldwide. The origin of ecotourism as a field in Colombia can be traced back to the early 1908s. Ecotourism has been hampered by corruption and pseudo-ecotourism based industries that focus on making large economic revenues that are not environmentally sound. Ecotourism research has been carried on a regional and local level in the Amazonas, Cundinamarca and Boyacá States among other regions. Currently, few research organizations are involved in ecotourism and few offer reliable plans for ecotourists. Recently, research in wetland ecotourism has provided elements to construct a reliable wetland restoration and conservation framework. This ecotourism framework provides the first opportunity to consistently manage wetland sites and propose real solutions to these highly threatened ecosystems. This chapter focuses on the recent and past advances on the field of ecotourism in Colombia. It explores ecotourism related aspects in the context of philosophy, biodiversity, culture, research, policy, education, ethics, conflict related aspects.

Chapter 5 – Studies have found that marine tourists can cause impact to the underwater environment by breaking corals and disturbing coral-associated benthic organisms. However, which type of dive tourists inflicts the most harm on the marine ecosystem? Few studies are able to throw light into this. Making use of data from the direct observation of diving behaviour and self-reported findings on the environmental attitudes and values of 80 Hong Kong divers, this chapter brings to light factors or attributes that would affect or associate with divers" underwater behaviour. It was found that by carrying a camera, divers made 9.8 more intended contacts per dive. Divers who are not so willing to avoid using non-biodegradable shampoos (a pro-environment behaviour) would also make more contacts on the marine biota. However, even the more disciplined divers in the sample are not so willing to financially contribute to marine conservation. On the whole, attitudinal and value-based variables can only explain about 20% of the variations in their underwater behaviour. Given existing findings, it is advisable to the underwater tourism industry to not just educate but also impose dive guide intervention to reduce divers" intended contacts on marine biota to protect the already stressful underwater environment.

Chapter 6 – This chapter focuses on the selection and use of sustainability indicators in the field of tourism. First, the authors begin by drawing up the context that makes the use of indicators an important approach in the management of sustainable tourism. Second, they address three main issues related to the use of sustainability indicators in tourism studies: i) the trade-off between the scientific and political approaches; ii) the potential role of indicators in tourism development policy planning, and iii) the interpretation of the indicators" score following their calculation. Finally, the authors discuss the implications of these proposals on research and public policy.

In: Ecotourism
Editor: Shannon C. Brophy

ISBN: 978-1-63482-027-1
© 2015 Nova Science Publishers, Inc.

Chapter 1

MAKING TOURISM MORE SUSTAINABLE: THE ROLE OF ECOTOURISM AND OF OTHER FORMS OF GREEN TOURISM

Francisco A. Serrano-Bernardo[*1], *Luigi Bruzzi*[2], *Marianna Marcucci*[2], *Alessandra Bonoli*[2] *and José Luis Rosúa-Campos*[1]

[1]Department of Civil Engineering. ETSI Caminos, Canales y Puertos. University of Granada. Granada, Spain
[2]Department of Civil, Chemical, Environmental and Materials Engineering. Facoltà di Ingegneria. University of Bologna. Bologna, Italy

ABSTRACT

The main objective of this article is the analysis of tourism activities located in a given territory during their evolution and steady state life. Interventions to make tourism more sustainable are deeply analysed. Specific tools to improve sustainability of tourism are also discussed. Positive effects induced by regulated procedures such as SEA, EIA, EMAS, ISO14001, ECOLABEL, SWOT ANALYSIS are taken into consideration as well. Specific attention is devoted to the implementation of the EU Ecolabel in sustainable hotel management. Some other forms

* Corresponding author E-mail: fserber@ugr.es

of environmental friendly sustainable tourism are also described. This paper discusses positive results expected from various kinds of sustainable tourism in terms of reduction of resource consumption, pollutants and CO_2 emissions, solid waste management, preservation of biodiversity, etc. Much attention is given to indicators able to measure sustainability of tourism in a given territory, such as economic performance (Gross Domestic Product, GDP), quality of social life (Human Development Index, HDI), health conditions (Life Expectancy at birth), energy consumption, air and water quality, etc. More specific indicators directly connected with tourism are also investigated. Among them, one can mention specific indicators such as the amount of green area per person, number of hotels, number of rooms and residences for families, traffic congestion and noise, etc. Specific case studies are devoted to the life of tourism destinations according to the model developed by Butler. In the last part of the study the characterization of the area and the calculation of the specific indicators are described. The methodology is tested and applied to some specific areas with the aim at showing the dynamic nature of the destination life divided among different phases. For the selected destinations, adequate indicators are identified and quantified with the aim of improving the level of sustainability of different conditions.

1. INTRODUCTION

Tourism is defined as the set of activities of persons travelling to and staying for the sake of rest, leisure, culture, health, etc. in places that are outside their usual environment for a period not exceeding one year [1]. Tourism is a response to numerous instances including: willingness to explore new environmental realities; need to rest, relax and care for their own health, travel to places of religious worship and visit places of great interest from the point of view of nature or art [2, 3]. Tourism deals with the movement of people in space and time, outside of their usual residence. At the heart of the tourism experience is therefore the tourist. The World Tourism Organization (UNWTO) defines tourism as the activity of people travelling/staying in countries other than their normal place of residence and outside of their everyday environment, for a period of at least 1 night but not more than one year, driven by reasons of curiosity, relaxation, business or pleasure [4] Tourism is an umbrella term that covers unclear boundaries including the conditions and phenomena related to people who are travelling, whatever reason that brings them to move [5]. Highly dependent on the quality of the place where it grows, the tourism sector is based on the sale of positive experiences and thus aims at ensuring a good experience, mainly based on the beauty of the landscape and cultural heritage, cleanliness of nature, good services and profitable business activities [6]. These elements and persons connected with them (workers, tourists and local residents) are the potential resources of the tourism industry. Tourism is a sector of the economy extremely rich that can also finance major events [7]; its development has experienced a nearly constant growth since the Second World War [8] with moments of decline resulting in international contingency as the attacks of September 11, 2001. The rise of tourism has been one of the main economic and social phenomenon of the twentieth century; it had an increase of about 25% over the past 25 years. Today it accounts for about 10% of economic activity in the world and is one of the main generators of employment [9, 10].

Despite being one of the oldest existing industries, tourism has become an important pillar for the majority of nations, as it contributes tangibly to their economic and social development. However, we cannot forget the obvious effects that it brings on natural environment and on the well-being and culture of the host population [11]. With the increase of tourist pressure and the over-exploitation of natural resources all the living species are deteriorated [12]. Within this complex framework, tourism is undergoing to a high risk in terms of environmental, cultural, social and economic effects that can no longer be ignored. For these reasons, tourism and its implications deserve careful consideration by all citizens, institutions and industry. Tourism produces an important benefit to the economy of a city, a region and whole country. As a result, the development of this sector can generate a significant contribution to the improvement of conditions in a territory. It is much more than a purely economic factor and this is the reason why is studied from many points of view [13]. There are countless reasons to develop tourism. First, it plays an important role in contributing to economic growth, improving its revenues, creating jobs, establishing regional and international relations, increasing productivity and income. Its expansion has a significant influence on the demand for some goods, such as transport and related infrastructures and services, employing skilled workforce. This is a great benefit to the local community or nation concerned, since it gets obvious benefits from high quality infrastructure, ease of access to certain areas and increased employment opportunities [14]. There are various types of tourism: cultural, gastronomic, natural, congress, therapeutic, spa, sports, entertainment, relaxation and rest, free time (leisure), and so on. Tourism can then be promoted in many ways such as through events, festivals, shows, fairs, etc.

There is no country in the world that does not have a tourism potential [15, 16]. There are even cases where tourism has been completely created from scratch thanks to man-made attractions; there are several types of attraction for example, gaming (gambling in Las Vegas) and prostitution (Brazil and Thailand) that are associated with established forms of tourism that require special controls. It follows, therefore, that the development of tourism, although it is not simple, it is practically possible everywhere. Tourism can contribute, often in a very clear and incisive way, to the diversification of productive activities that can generate more goods and/or services being produced and offered [17]. This is of particular importance as it broadens the effects on its economy: it is understood that the more the economy is diversified, then the system appears to be "protected" and thus free from risk [18]. Extending this concept to the tourism sector, there is a diversification of services and products offered introducing different forms of tourism within the same territory.

These paper only analyses the different forms of tourism, paying particular attention to the types of tourism that adopt measures to improve sustainability. Not discussed are the effects normally expected from climate change that can be encountered in destinations located on the coast that could be subject to extensive damage caused by the sea level rise [19]. Much attention is given instead to the life cycle of a destination and to the life cycle of a holiday highlighting the importance of energy consumption in the entire cycle, especially in transportation.

2. TOURISM MARKET

The expansion of tourism took place mainly during the last 50 years, leading it to become a true global industry. The growth was due primarily to three factors: 1) the increase in personal income and leisure time, 2) improved transportation systems and 3) increased knowledge about unknown parts of the world thanks to the more efficient communication. The European tourism is the world leader in the number of arrivals and overnight stays [10]: it covers 1/2 of the world demand. The Mediterranean is the number one tourist destination in the world. It is expected that international arrivals will exceed approximately 1.4 billion in 2020 (Figure 1). The tourism analysed by region shows that by around 2020 the first three geographical areas in terms of arrivals will be Europe, East Asia, the Pacific and the Americas [20].

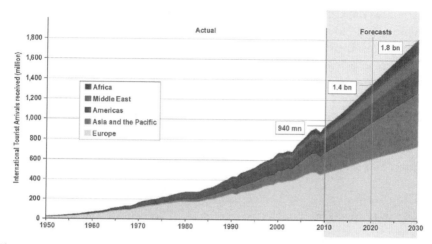

Figure 1. Evolution of tourism in the period 1950-2030. Source: [10].

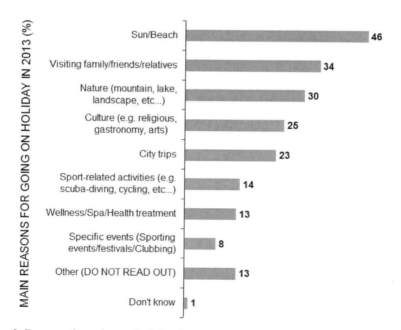

Figure 2. Reasons for going on holiday for Europeans in 2013 (2014). Source: [22]. Base: 50% from total number of respondents-EU28 (those who went on a personal travel for a minimum of four consecutive nights during 2013).

From this data it appears that tourism is one of the strongest sectors of the economies of the Member States of the European Union: the tourist activities in these States involve about a large number of enterprises; In 2014 they generate up to 9.1% of GDP; 10,1% of total employment [21]. All these figures are moreover expected to increase, because tourism demand will not cease to grow.

The growth of tourism is motivated by the already mentioned considerations: increase in personal income; improvement of transport means; more information on the destinations with high attractiveness. The reasons expressed by Europeans to undertake tourism activities are shown in Figure 2 [22].

Tourism, including connected activity, is one of the main industrial activities in terms of the production of wealth in the world. The employees in direct and indirect activities are numbered at more than 300 million and profitability amounts almost to 10% of the world GDP [23]. Between 1990 and 2015, tourists worldwide increased from 450 million to 1 billion (Figure 1). It is estimated that, in the world today, people employed in tourism activities (direct) are 103 million, or 3.4% of the entire labour force [22].

3. THE ROLE OF TOURISM IN ECONOMIC, SOCIAL AND ENVIRONMENTAL FRAMEWORK

Tourism is a key factor in the economic and social development of the local community; if well managed, can produce jobs and improve the management of natural and cultural heritage [24, 25]. A question that often arises is: Can tourism and the environment coexist? In fact, tourism activities may adversely affect the environmental quality of the area; the heavy tourist traffic can lead to deterioration of the physical and morphological landscape and may cause a progressive increase in the levels of pollution of air, water and noise [26, 27].

Many tourist activities are concentrated in a few months a year, typically the summer months, and this is a further critical element related to the concentration in space and time of seasonal factors due to anthropic pressure. The various type of tourism including different conditions of use are: summer tourism, seaside tourism; skiing in the winter months and cultural and religious tourism throughout the year. The expected results are very different from each other and include the use of tourism as leisure time, cultural and environmental interest, scientific curiosity, and so on. However, we should not forget that tourism is a major consumer of resources, especially energy and water [28]; it is also a booming business and this reinforces concerns about the ability to manage it in a sustainable way.

With the increase in demand, tourist facilities have developed and are now within the reach of a large number of tourists; however, beach tourists are no longer asking only for sun, sand and sea, but are demanding alternative range of activities. For residents who live in tourism area there is the problem of preserving the identity of their territory. Among the different forms of tourism of this kind, we can mention ski tourism, cultural tourism, eco-tourism, religious tourism, culinary tourism and agritourism.

A large part of tourism developing in the Mediterranean basin can be called Cultural Tourism, where a tourist can find a wealth of local cultural heritage regarding history, art works, art and religion [29, 30]. Cultural tourism is concentrated mostly in cities where there are museums and theatres of the past. You can also consider the cultural folklore offered to tourists in the form of dance, music, theatre, eno-gastronomy inspired by local traditions. Recently, international organizations have stressed the importance of cultural tourism for regional development. A form of tourism that is being developed is dedicated to the health and well-being: in this case, the tourist finds facilities that provide specific medical treatments, physiotherapy, rehabilitation and so on [31-33].

In Mediterranean area, many valuable aspects are concentrated such as sea and beaches, mountains, landscapes, etc. This is a matter of movement of tourists in that area: this unfortunately entails increasing human pressure that threatens fragile ecosystems and produces the degradation of natural and artistic heritage. The risks that the Mediterranean area/region runs, due to the pressures of tourism, includes the shortage of resources and an increasing population, that is already over 150 million inhabitants, doubling in the last 25 years; tourist arrivals are at about 300 million [34]; one of the critical issues that requires a discontinuous management of resources and services. Tourism in the Mediterranean is also affected by a progressive trend towards mass tourism, which undoubtedly makes the market more affordable, but an element of pressure on the environment.

The impact that tourism can potentially create requires managing tourism in a sustainable way. Sustainable tourism is defined as a type of tourism that meets the needs of the tourists and at the same time facilitate measures to protect and improve the tourism opportunities for future generations [25]. In other words, the management should be sustainable from environment-tal, economic, ethical and social point of view. Ecologically sustainable management of tourism requires preserving the natural and cultural heritage, promoting the interest of tourists toward environmental characteristics of the destination, using efficiently resources (water and energy). A socially sustainable management of tourism requires engaging and informing all categories of the public; promoting experiences at the destination; promoting the curiosity of tourists to local realities; developing the awareness of tourists towards the local population.

An economically sustainable management of tourism requires recognizing its important role for the implementation of environmental policy, planning and land management [35]. It is therefore necessary to become aware of the limits of the tourist activity the so called carrying capacity; tourism should also be able to develop activities generating financial gain for the local population and making residents self-sufficient economically. In other words, tourism should be able to:

- preserve resources for future generations;
- maintain productivity of resources;
- conserve biodiversity;
- avoid irreversible changes in ecosystems;
- ensure equity between and within generations;
- maintain and protect the identity of the destination, the region and the nation.

To measure the level of sustainability specific indicators are needed such as the consumption of water and energy; the amount of waste produced; the number of tourists accommodated; the number of occupied rooms; the surface of green areas; consumption of water and energy in particular areas (laundries, kitchens, golf courses, swimming pools and restaurants).

4. SUSTAINABLE AND GREEN TOURISM

For the purposes of contributing to environmental protection, there is an increasing market for so-called eco-tourism that is practiced by people of the middle class who are interested in living the tourist experience in contact with the nature [36]. This is limited to a small number of individuals; an excessive number of individuals in ecotourism destinations could compromise the integrity of the natural environment. Tourism can also assume an additional meaning by directing its business activities in the direction of so-called green economy. This approach is based on increased investment in green technologies, increase in employment in green sectors; increase in the contribution to GDP of green products; decrease in consumption of energy and resources (water), reduction of CO_2 and pollutant emissions; reduction of waste production (per unit of GDP) [37].

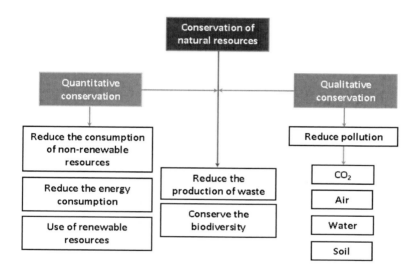

Figure 3. Improving sustainability through conservation of natural resources. Source: [39].

A schematic of an approach to improve sustainability is shown in Figure 3. The approach is based on resource conservation both qualitative and quantitative; the pathway toward improved sustainability is schematically shown in the figure. Tourism, such as any other human activity, can improve its sustainability through the extensive use of renewable resources, the use of closed-loop processes with reduced consumption of energy and resources; moreover, the production of waste should be limited, the service life of commercial products extended, emissions of liquid and gaseous pollutants reduced [38]. The reduced consumption of resources, such as water and energy, and the reduced impact that tourism can have on the fragile ecosystems of the area, will make the achievement of an acceptable level of sustainability easier.

ENVIRONMENTAL PROTECTION: TOOLS, PREVENTION AND MANAGEMENT		
TOOLS	EXPECTED RESULTS	OBTAINED RESULTS
Environmental Impace Assessment (EIA)	Prevention of environmental effects in the preliminary phase of a project	Prevention of environmental effects
Environmental Management System (EMS)	Continuous improvement on environmental performance	Proper environmental management
Life Cycle Assessment (LCA)	Assessment of environmental effects in the stages of life of a product	Conservation on natural resources
Remediation	Removal/isolation of pollutants through chemical or biological processes	Remediation of contaminated sites

Figure 4. Prevention and management tools for sustainable tourism. Source: [39].

The common goal of all the programs dealing with tourism activities is to reach an adequate level of sustainability capable of satisfying social needs without compromising the environmental quality of the concerned area. Local institutions play an important role in planning and managing tourism not only for their institutional duties, but also as a role model regarding environmental policies. The tools provided by the regulations offer an effective support to sustainability (Figure 4). Initial planning of the area and its development are necessary conditions for preserving the quality of the landscape and ensuring an appropriate use of natural and cultural resources. The tools provided by European regulations offer opportunities to preserve the prevalent vocation and the valuable characteristics of the area. The tools include the Strategic Environmental Assessment (SEA) and the Environmental Management Systems (EMS) like EMAS and ISO 14001, which are applicable to different public and private organizations in the area [39]. For tourism services, there is also the Ecolabel that is expressly directed at hotels and campsites. A systematic use of such tools would result in an overall improvement in the sustainability of the whole area. It must be remembered that the development and spatial planning of tourism activities may have further improvements by appropriate public opinion surveys measuring the level of sustainability by means of adequate indicators such as the ecological footprint and the carbon footprint [40, 41].

The carrying capacity is an important indicator [42-45]: monitoring it in terms of number of individuals per km^2 can reveal if the resources are starting to become scarce or the area shows signs of ecological stress. Under these conditions, there may be a crisis and the subsequent collapse of the area with consequences that may result in damage to local ecosystems.

Among the numerous environmental indicators [46-48], some are specific to the area where tourism is developed. The data shown in Figure 5 shows an example of indicators for seaside tourism in the city of Cervia (Italy) [3].

ENVIRONMENTAL INDICATORS	UNITS	CERVIA VALUE	ITALIAN VALUE
Pedestrian area	m^2/inhabitant	2.1	0.18
Limited traffic zone	m^2/inhabitant	16.1	2.5
Cycle lines	m/inhabitant	0.5	0.1
Available green area	m^2/inhabitant	110	10
Motorization rate	car/inhabitant	0.62	0.56
Ecological municipality vehicles	% on total	29%	--
Parking place	place/inhabitant	0.15	--
Natural gas consumption	m^3/inh. year	1384	--
Water consumption	litres/inh. die	450	325
Waste collected	kg/inh. year	1089	539
Selected waste collection	% on total	38%	20%

Figure 5. Sustainability indicatoris for Cervia IER in 2007. Source: [3].

The analysis focused on the aspects that most affected the conditions typical of the summer season. To measure the ability of a territory to be the correct location for particular tourism activities, it is necessary to conduct a preliminary analysis. The area should be characterized by identifying its potential for tourism. In this phase, vocational aspects and the related characteristics such as natural, social, economic and cultural factors are investigated. This process allows qualifying the destination in terms of being able to satisfy the sustainability of the area and the expectations of tourists. Characteristics of social nature, such as the residents" ability to develop planning and managing programs are also examined; this is done by collecting and analysing the needs of services and resources to meet the expectations of the tourists without compromising the possible contribution of the residents. The eventual expansion of tourism in terms of carrying capacity is estimated in order to obtain a trend line that anticipates any developing environmental crisis. In a second phase, the focus is addressed to assessing the degree of satisfaction of the tourists towards the area during their stay in it. This analysis is based on using questionnaires, which highlight the type of satisfaction (art, local culture, nature, landscape, sun, sea, mountains, etc.). The questions deal with the reasons why the tourists want to visit the area, with the degree of satisfaction based on age, sex, nationality and level of education of the tourists who visit the area. Other questions deal with the frequency with which they visit the territory, level of satisfaction of facilities existing in the area, means of transportation used to reach the tourist destination, level of satisfaction of conditions of the area, including rate of overcrowding, air and noise pollution, traffic congestion, pedestrian zones, bicycle lanes. The analysis could also estimate the level of satisfaction of tourists and residents in comparison with other tourist areas (national, local). Tourism management highlights the need to collect a large amount of data for it and to be used to develop a sound environmental, social and economic policy. The collected data to be effective, require analyses based on reliable and tested statistical methods.

The ecotourism or green tourism is a form of sustainable tourism, focused on the discovery and preservation of nature and ecosystems; it includes also agritourism, rural tourism and urban ecology (ecological gardens, ecological green spaces etc.) [49, 50]. Ecotourism‛s main objective is to discover and preserve different forms of natural resources such as fascinating landscapes, local flora and fauna (e.g., various types of forests, lions or elephants, observation and study on birds or whales), while respecting ecosystems, even helping to restore, in a voluntary approach. The ecotourism activity generally involves fundamentals of education and interpretation that could help to raise awareness of the need to preserve natural and cultural capital [51]. Ecotourism has a positive environmental impact and contributes to the well-being of local population. Ecotourism is a means to enhance biodiversity that is in contrast to mass tourism that degrades the natural environment; this is possible by incorporating an ethical and environmentally aware dimension [52, 53]. A question can arise when you try to diversify sustainable tourism from ecotourism. The term "Sustainable tourism" generally describes all forms of tourism that respect and preserve cultural, social and natural heritage of a territory focusing the attention of tourists on the nature of the site with the result of minimizing the negative impact they could generate [50]. Having these considerations in mind, ecotourism is an important part of sustainable tourism; it can facilitate the discovery of ecosystems, of agro or ethno-cultural aspects of biodiversity. More specifically it is a type of tourism that ensures sustainable economic development in the long term, whilst being respectful of environmental and socio-cultural resources [54].

There are other types of tourism under the umbrella of sustainable and green tourism one of which is the rural tourism, this type is practiced in areas where agritourism is also popular or possible [55, 56]. Rural tourism poses particular problems in areas where the land is essentially private, and where domestic animals or crops can sometimes suffer from scarce professional preparation with these aspects of rural life tourists. There is also another form and it is called hunting tourism. These two practices are often a source of clashes and difficulties in the management of security, especially for walking/hiking routes in the woods or on the edge of forests. Winter tourism with winter sports can also generate significant environmental impacts through bad tourism planning, space consumption, deforestation for creating ski slopes, diversion of water resources, etc. [57, 58].

5. THE LIFE CYCLE OF A TOURIST DESTINATION - BUTLER MODEL

In 1980, Richard W Butler a Canadian geographer presented a model [59] showing the life cycle of a tourist destination (Tourism Area Life Cycle, TALC). He argues that a destination follows a life cycle consisting of several phases of development, each one distinct from the others. The phases are characterized by a different trend in demand and offer. TALC is suitable for any tourist area describing the dynamic process and its evolution over time. Its purpose is to draw attention to the dynamic nature of the destination and to propose a generalized process of development, in order to counteract the potential decline through targeted interventions and solvers (planning, management and development).

The model is based on the idea that tourism is sensitive to the environmental characteristics (natural beauty, landscapes, cultures, etc.). However, tourism can put a strain on the land and its resources: the process of development and management of tourism tends to "eat" the allocate resources. According to Butler, the use of resources is strictly connected to the concept of carrying capacity. It is therefore necessary to identify the limiting factors (e.g., litres of water/day person, capacity for wastewater treatment, square meters of beach per person, square meters of public parks per person). UNWTO defines tourism carrying capacity as *"the maximum number of people that may visit a tourist destination at the same time, without causing destruction of the physical, economic, socio-cultural environment and an unacceptable decrease in the quality of visitors' satisfaction"* [60].

If the carrying capacity is exceeded, the tourist area is likely to decline: this area will become less competitive and attractive, leading to a drop in tourists, investment and development. To reduce the danger of reaching the stage of decline, a number of actions are introduced to avoid reaching or exceeding the different load capacities (economic, socio-cultural and environmental) of the area or, if possible, to increase the load capacity of the same, in order to meet the increasing demand. Figure 6 shows the evolution of the life cycle of a tourist destination along the lines defined by Butler [59].

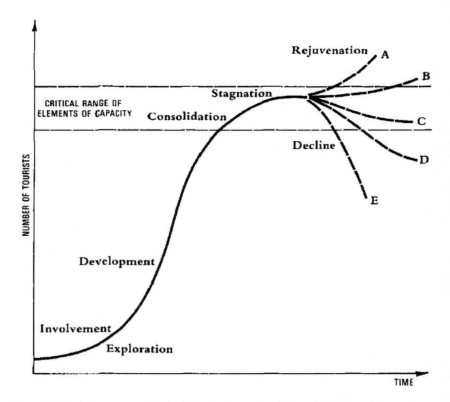

Figure 6. Typical representation of the Butler model (Hypothetical evolution of a tourist area). Source: [59].

According to [59], tourism development begins with a spontaneous exploratory phase of the future tourist destination, characterized by the arrival of a low number of tourists, defined as "pioneers" because of difficult access and lack of receptivity of the destination. At this stage, the contact with the local community is very intense. This is not a real tourism due to the lack of any form of organization of the offer (the infrastructure is almost non-existent), except for some spontaneous initiative aimed at providing basic services for visitors. At this time, the impact on the area is almost irrelevant. Then there is the phase of the involvement, in which the local population begins to glimpse the economic potential of tourism; first forms of organization, although still rudimentary, are starting to develop. In this phase, some simple tourism activities (especially hospitality and restoration managed by family members) are springing up, together with increased opportunities for income and employment. The promotion of the site and the construction of appropriate infrastructure are beginning in order to reduce the difficulties encountered by visitors to reach the destination. It is in this stage that the destination develops a real market area, with defined space and time distribution (seasonality). The next stage is the development stage that is the most crucial moment of the entire route. From this time on and the manner in which this occurs depends the fate of a tourist resort and the success or failure of policies. At this stage, outside organizations come into play, which gradually will replace local initiatives. The public sector provides with incisive input for infrastructure investments such as roads, water and energy supplies and other basic services. At the same time, promotional activities are developing at national and international level. At this stage, due to the increased awareness of the area, there is a large increase in the annual growth rate of visitors, reaching a seasonal peak that can reach 2-3 times the number of residents. In terms of employment, tourism and migration attracts commuters from the surrounding region, as it is no longer sufficient to rely on local labour force due to the substantial increase in tourists. When the exploitation of the touristic area reaches its maximum, two factors are joining: the maximum utilization of resources creates heavy impacts; the historical and natural landscape is largely replaced by the modern urban landscape. At this point there is a significant increase in foreign capital. After this stage of development begins the consolidation phase that represents a further critical phase for the carrying capacity: the number of arrivals continues to increase, although at a lower rate than previously. It is for this reason that it becomes necessary to adopt measures to prolong the tourist season. The site has attained a specialization in tourism so that tends to establish itself as the main economic activity of the area, but this fact has consequences. The first symptoms of environmental disease appear with degenerative damage to the environment. Earliest forms of opposition from the local population towards tourism and its consequences are beginning. At the same time, congestion and environmental degradation tend to alienate the most rewarding segments of the demand. Therefore, it is needed to create a hierarchy of spaces devoted to tourism with real tourist districts. Going to the stage of stagnation, the number of arrivals, once peaked, slowly begins to decline. There is a decline in demand in terms of quality that is oriented toward a progressive increase of organized mass tourism. There is also the creation of artificial structures. This changes completely the image of the destination that loses more and more the original characteristics of the area. It is the time when excessive pressure of tourism leads to the overcoming of the various thresholds imposed by the carrying capacity of an area, stimulating a strong opposition among citizens towards tourism. In fact, the creation of artificial things makes the image of the destination depending less and less on the characteristics of the place.

Decline creeps in, which marks the loss of competitiveness of the destination against the other and maybe newer tourist destinations: the number of arrivals decreases rapidly and the standard of quality of supplied services drops considerably. This stage may continue to the ultimate final exit from the tourist market, although it is very likely that the local authorities, at this point, try to remedy the situation and revitalize the tourism industry and the image of the area through a series of rejuvenation measures. This could lead to an eventual recovery position, temporary or permanent, through the implementation of tourism policies aimed at creating new motivations for travel and overnight stays, as well as direct supply to various demand segments (e.g., creating new attractions complementary to artificial nature or exploiting resources hitherto neglected).

The Butler model is extremely versatile since it can be applied to individual accommodation units, to geographic areas or tourist destinations both as a method of analysis on "healthy" tourism and as a tool for strategic planning of the actions to undertake [61-63]. In many cases, there are limitations: first, we must emphasize that the approach is a generalization, as not all places will follow this process. Richard W Butler also asserts that each case is different and therefore requires the adaptation of the model to match the reality of the investigated area. Limitations are also due to a likely discontinuity in the collection of data over long periods [62]. The model also does not take into account a number of more subsequent stages in the development that could possibly occur: each destination, in fact, after development, seems to propose different situations. Finally, the parameter of the arrivals will not be considered in its entirety but only in a representative way, i.e., without taking into account the composition of demand, average length of stay and other quality traits. In any case, one cannot fail to highlight the benefits brought by this model. Its application appears suitable to a recently built city. Young destinations, in fact, based on the application of this theory, could figure out in advance the risks of a possible decline in the future. Therefore, they could prevent a spontaneous uncontrolled growth, aim to stabilize the levels consistent with strategies for medium and long term. For the destinations that rely on fragile resources (eco-tourism, archaeological tourism, etc.) it could be envisaged to have development plans that limit and monitor potential booms in order to maintain just in time the potential of attraction. The spontaneous development, in fact, often leads to sometimes catastrophic results, by exceeding the carrying capacity of a destination that deteriorate the original resources, factors that would lead in the long run to a predictable and inevitable decline [64].

6. TOURISM AND TRAVEL: ENERGY AND ENVIRONMENTAL COST OF A HOLIDAY

To complete the analysis of the effects due to tourism and to assess the possibility of creating a sustainable tourism, it is necessary to introduce the concept of tourism life cycle. Tourism requires that people move from where they live to a tourist destination; this movement is accomplished by many different means: car, bus, train, plane, boat, etc. Almost all the vehicles need fuel (mainly fossil) that produce large amounts of CO_2 [38]. The total amount of CO_2 produced for a whole life cycle is the sum of the quantities produced during the various phases of the cycle. The phases having the largest environmental effect are transport, tourist accommodation services (hotels, private houses, residences), supply of consumer goods, etc. For the movement tourists utilize different means of transportation: automobile and airplane are now readily available to everyone and are used intensively for tourism. At a global level tourism is now at such a significant level that the energy used is a considerable part of the total global energy consumption (5%); were as the largest contribution (40%) comes from aviation [38].

Greenhouse gases emitted in a typical tourism activity (e.g., a holiday) are resulting from the round-trip journey and the on site electricity consumption for lighting, air conditioning, heat pumps and appliances [65, 66]. To reduce fossil energy consumption in tourism on site effective use of renewable energy and energy saving measures can be helpful. Reducing the energy consumption required for transport is a difficult task especially if travel is made by airplane. This could be achieved by reducing the use of airplanes, but this could be very detrimental to the development of tourism: a measure to reduce greenhouse gas emissions from air travel is to avoid as much as possible intermediate stops, thus reducing fuel consumption during take-off and landing. Further savings can also occur by adopting innovative technologies. The summer season is the most critical time for the resorts. The environmental impact (particularly CO_2 emissions) of a holiday is due mainly to transport plus the demand generated in the host structures [38, 67].

As previously mentioned, energy consumption in tourism is a significant percent of the total global energy consumption (5%): the bulk of this consumption (40%) is due to air transport for tourism, 32% travel by car and 22 % consumption at the destination [68]. Tourism, therefore, is an energy intensive consumer, not so much due to the consumption of fuel and electricity at the destination, but due to the high consumption of fuel for travelling (Figure 7).

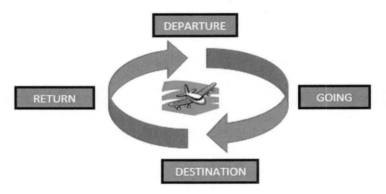

Figure 7. Schematic picture of round-trip travel for a holiday in a tourist destination.

The distance travelled to reach a tourist destination is far from negligible and can range from a few hundred kilometres to thousands of kilometres. Holidays at long distance destinations are on the rise because transport is becoming faster, cheaper and more comfortable. The role of air travel is increasingly important since tourists are more attracted to the exotic and extremes to be found at these long distance destinations.

The graph in Figure 8 clearly confirms that the airplane is the largest producer of CO_2, especially if you fly shorter distances even when there is no stop. When the flight distance is higher, then there is a significant decrease in specific emissions as the take-off and landing portion of the journey is smaller when compared to the complete journey time. Cars, trains and busses, all have lower emissions than airplanes. The decrease in specific consumption of fuel is the most effective measure to reduce emissions of the various means of transportations [69]; this is an ongoing process for the car and is a target for aircraft [70-72]. To comply with these requirements, the planes must increase the number of passengers flying long distances without stops. The energy consumption for tourism and its mobility is growing and this causes significant environmental impacts, as well as high costs [73].

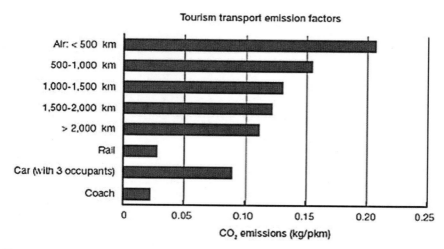

Figure 8. Specific emissions of CO_2 (kg/passenger km) from different transportation means. Source: [68].

As for energy consumption in the destination, there are considerable possible savings by converting to renewable energy and introducing energy saving measures. The major problem remains the reduction in emissions in air travel [74]. The air traffic is particularly suited to the needs of tourism; but unfortunately has high fuel consumption that penalizes the cost and environmental impact especially due to the considerable emissions of greenhouse gases [75]. A hypothetical and substantial reduction in air travel favouring the car, train, boat and bus would not be able to meet the demands of tourism, which requires quick trips even for long distances [76]. Therefore, to overcome these difficulties are being developed specific technological solutions able to reduce the environmental cost in terms of CO_2 emissions per passenger and per kilometre [38, 77]. The latest solutions require large aircraft with a seating capacity of more than 800 passengers. Therefore, the emission factors can be further reduced if the distance covered is over 2000 kilometres (better results are reached with for non-stop flights of 10.000 km or more) and the number of passengers is high for a single aircraft. At the moment only two aircraft are available with these characteristics and they are the Airbus A380 and Boeing 787. Both have performance figures that are competitive with the other forms of transport. They have a low fuel consumption (3.5 litres/100 passenger km) and reasonable specific emissions (30 g CO_2/passenger km). In particular, the Airbus A380 has four turbofan engines, can accommodate 853 passengers on board in economy configuration and its specific fuel consumption is comparable to that of a modern car with high efficiency. The next generation of aircraft through the use of new technologies can boast lower emissions further (3 litres/100 passenger km), equal to those of a modern high-efficiency diesel car with three people on board (26 g/passenger km).

CONCLUSION

All tourist activities generate significant environmental impact, which may increase because tourists tend to go farther and more often. In addition, the World Tourism Organization estimates that between 2000 and 2020, tourism is expected to grow by about 10% and that Europe could experience a doubling of international arrivals. The European Union aims to fix some general guidelines for the development of tourism; therefore it is helpful to follow the approach recommended by the European Union for Agenda 21, which is summarized in the following four points:

- Prevent and reduce territorial and environmental impacts of tourism at destinations;
- Controlling the growth of tourism-related transport and its negative effects on the environment;
- Encourage a favourable local sustainable development controlled by the tourism stakeholders;
- Promoting responsible tourism as an important factor in social and cultural development.

To prevent and reduce environmental impact due to tourism it is important to accurately plan the involved territory by following the approach of European tools such as Environmental Impact Assessment and Strategic Environmental Assessment. Moreover, attention should be paid to the conservation of the identity of the area by vitalizing traditions, gastronomy, landscapes. The production of CO_2 at the destination can be reduced by generating energy by renewables and energy saving, but the most important action is the reduction of use of fossil fuels. To achieve this task is difficult since the long distance transportation for tourism is becoming very popular. To develop sustainable tourism the role of residents and stakeholders is critical. The most significant local stakeholders are agencies, information services (guides, chaperones), researchers (universities) and other research bodies such as: governments and their agencies, tourism observatories, chamber of commerce and industry, social partners, industries involved (hotels/accommodation), catering, leisure, culture, transport, tour operators and travel organizations, consultants, consumer groups, users, financial institutions, banks and insurance companies.

ACKNOWLEDGMENTS

We thank Mr. Philip Dudley for the English revision of the manuscript.

REFERENCES

[1] Stylidis, D., Biran, A., Sit, J., & Szivas, E. M. (2014). Residents" support for tourism development: The role of residents" place image and perceived tourism impacts. *Tourism Management, 45*, 260-274.

[2] Jamal, T., & Hill, S. (2004). Developing a framework for indicators of authenticity: the place and space of cultural and heritage tourism. *Asian Pacific Journal of Tourism Research*, 9 (4), 353-372.

[3] Bruzzi, L., Boragno, V., Serrano-Bernardo, F. A., Verità, S., & Rosúa-Campos, J. L. (2011). Environmental management policy in a coastal tourism municipality: the case study of Cervia (Italy). *Local Environment,* 16 (2), 93-113.

[4] UNWTO (United Nations World Tourism Organization) (2010). International recommendations for tourism statistics 2008. Department of Economic and Social Affairs, Series M No. 83/Rev.1, New York: United Nations.

[5]   Marcucci, M. (2014). Gestione sostenibile del turismo - due realtà a confronto: la Repubblica di San Marino e il comprensorio di Granada (Spagna). Tesi di laurea magistrale. Università di Bologna (Italia)

[6]   Tang, Z. (2015). An integrated approach to evaluating the coupling coordination between tourism and the environment. *Tourism Management*, 46, 11-19.

[7]   Hedlund, T. (2011). The impact of values, environmental concern, and willingness to accept economic sacrifices to protect the environment on tourists" intentions to buy ecologically sustainable tourism alternatives. *Tourism and Hospitality Research*, 11 (4), 278-288

[8]   Huybers, T., & Bennett, J. (2003). Environmental management and the competitiveness of nature-based tourism destinations. *Environmental and Resource Economics*, 24, 213-233

[9]   UNWTO (United Nations World Tourism Organization) (2014). UNWTO Tourism Barometer. October 2014-Volume 12 http://mkt. unwto.org/es/category/barometer-tags/barometer

[10]   UNWTO (United Nations World Tourism Organization) (2014). UNWTO Tourism Highlights: 2014 Edition http://mkt.unwto.org/ publication/unwto-tourism-highlights-2014-edition

[11]   Gössling, S., Hansson, C. B., Hörstmeier, O., & Saggel, S. (2002). Ecological footprint analysis as a tool to assess tourism sustainability. *Ecological Economics*, 43, 199-211.

[12]   Campbell, M. L., & Hewitt, C. L. (2006). A hierarchical framework to aid biodiversity assessment for coastal zone management and marine protected area selection. *Ocean & Coastal Management*, 49, 133-146.

[13]   Lee, S., & Jamal, T. (2008). Environmental justice and environmental equity in tourism: missing links to sustainability. *Journal of Ecotourism*, 7(1), 44-67.

[14]   Harrill, R. (2004). Residents" attitudes toward tourism development: a literature review with implications for tourism planning. *Journal of Planning Literature*, 18, 251-266.

[15]   Croes, R., & Kubickova, M. (2013). From potential to ability to compete: Towards a performance-based tourism competitiveness index. *Journal of Destination, Marketing & Management*, 2, 146-154.

[16]   Gabor, M. R., Contiu, L.C., & Oltean, F. V. (2012). A comparative analysis regarding European tourism competitiveness: emerging versus developed markets. *Procedia Economics and Finance*, 3, 361-366.

[17]   Lee, C. C., & Chang, C. P. (2008). Tourism development and economic growth: A closer look at panels. *Tourism Management*, 29, 180-192.

[18] Michelacci, C., & Schivardi, F. (2013). Does idiosyncratic business risk matter for growth?. *Journal of European Economic Association*, 11(2), 343-368.

[19] Gómez-Martín, M. B., Armesto-López, X. A., Cors-Iglesias, M., & Muñoz-Negrete, J. (2014). Adaptation strategies to climate change in the tourist sector: The case of coastal tourism in Spain. *Tourism-An International Interdisciplinary Journal*, 62(3), 293-308.

[20] Toureg Consortium (2010). Competitiveness and knowledge in the tourism sector. *DELIVERABLE 2.1:* Report of the Analysis of the situation of the services sector linked to tourism in the regions taking part in the project. Sector SWOT análisis. http://www.tourism innovation.eu

[21] WTT (World Travel and Tourism Council) (2014). Economic impact 2014: European Union. http://www.wttc.org/focus/research-for-action/ economic-impact-analysis/regional-reports/

[22] European Comission (2014). Preferences of Europeans towards tourism. Flash Eurobarometer 392-TNS Political & Social. Directorate-General for Enterprise and Industry. http://www.ec.europa.eu/public_opinion/ flash/fl_392_en.pdf

[23] WTT (World Travel and Tourism Council) (2014). Economic impact 2014: World. http://www.wttc.org/focus/research-for-action/economic-impact-analysis/regional-reports/

[24] Bramwell, B., & Lane, B. (1993). Sustaining tourism: An evolving global approach. *Journal of Sustainable Tourism*, 1(1), 1–5.

[25] Hardy, A., Beeton, R. J. S., & Pearson, L. (2002). Sustainable tourism: an overview of the concept and its position in relation to conceptualisations of tourism. *Journal of Sustainable Tourism*, 10(6), 475-496.

[26] Dubois, G., Peeters, P., Ceron, J.-P., & Gössling, S. (2011). The future tourism mobility of the world population: Emission growth versus climate policy. *Transportation Research Part A*, 45, 1031-1042.

[27] Roe, P., Hrymak, V., & Dimanche, F. (2014). Assessing environmental sustainability in tourism and recreation areas: a risk-assessment-based model. *Journal of Sustainable Tourism*, 22(2), 319-338.

[28] Kuo, N. W., & Chen, P. H. (2009). Quantifying energy use, carbon dioxide emission, and other environmental loads from island tourism based on a life cycle assessment approach. *Journal of Cleaner Production*, 17(15), 1324-1330

[29] Fournier, L.-S. (2008). Festivals, games, and ludic performances as a new potential intangible cultural heritage in the mediterranean world. *Journal of Mediterranean Studies*, 18(1), 1-15.

[30] Lowenthal, D. (2008). Mediterranean heritage: ancient marvel, modern millstone. *Nations and Nationalism*, 14(2), 369-392.

[31] Filep, S. (2014). Moving beyond subjective well-being: a tourism critique. *Journal of Hospitality & Tourism Research*, 38(2), 266-274.

[32] Koncul, N. (2012). Wellness: A new mode of tourism. *Ekonomska Istrazivanja*, 25(2), 525-534.

[33] Chang, L., Beisse-Zee, R. (2013) Consumer perception of healthfulness and appraisal of health-promoting tourist destinations. *Tourism Review*, 68(1), 34-47.

[34] WTT (World Travel and Tourism Council) (2014). Economic impact 2014: Mediterranean. http://www.wttc.org/focus/research-for-action/economic-impact-analysis/regional-reports/

[35] UNEP/WTO (United Nations Environment Programme and World Tourism Organization) (2005). Making tourism more sustainable: A guide for Policy Makers. UNEP/WTO: Paris.

[36] Fennell, D. A. (2015). Ecotourism (4th edition). Oxon-New York: Routledge.

[37] Delacy, T., Jiang, M., Lipman. G., & Vorster, S. (Eds.) (2014). Green growth and travelism: Concept, policy and practice for sustainable tourism. Oxon-New York: Routledge.

[38] Serrano-Bernardo, F., Bruzzi, L., Toscano, E.H., & Rosúa-Campos, J.L. (2012). Pollutants and greenhouse gases emissions produced by tourism life cycle: possible solutions to reduce emissions and to introduce adaptation measures. In B. Haryanto (Ed.), Air pollution: A comprehensive perspective (pp. 105-137). Rijeka, Croatia: InTech.

[39] Bruzzi, L., & Serrano-Bernardo, F. (2012). Concepto de sostenibilidad. In F. Serrano-Bernardo & L. Bruzzi (Eds.), Gestión sostenible del ambiente: Principios, contexto, métodos (1ª edición, pp. 45-76). Granada, España: Editorial Universidad de Granada-CLUEB.

[40] Wackernagel, M., & Rees, W. (1996). Our ecological footprint: Reducing Human Impact of Earth. Canada: New Society Publishers.

[41] Gössling, S. Carbon management in tourism: Mitigating the impacts on climate change. Oxon/New York: Routledge; 2011

[42] Kostopolou, S., & Kyritsis, I. (2006). A tourism carrying capacity indicator for protected areas. *Anatolia*, 17(1), 5-24.

[43] Navarro Jurado, E., Tejada Tejada, M., Almeida García, F., Cabello González, J., Cortés Macías, R., Delgado Peña, J., Fernández Gutiérrez, F., Gutiérrez Fernández, G., Luque Gallego, M., Málvarez García, G., Marcenaro Gutiérrez, O,. Navas Concha, F., Ruiz de la Rúa, F., Ruiz Sinoga, J., & Solís Becerra, F. (2012). Carrying capacity assessment for tourist destinations. Methodology for the creation of synthetic indicators applied in a coastal area. *Tourism Management*, 33, 1337-1346.

[44] ian, Y-n., Wang, H., & Hou, Z. (2012). Developing Resources Environmental Carrying Capacity Indicator System Based on Resource Environmental Problem Identification. *Advanced Materials Research*, 356-360, 734-737.

[45] Navarro Jurado, E., Damian, I. M., Fernández-Morales, A. (2013). Carrying capacity model applied in coastal destinations. *Annals of Tourism Research*, 43, 1-19.

[46] Miller, G. (2001). The development of indicators for sustainable tourism: results of a Delphi survey of tourism researchers. *Tourism Management*; 22, 351–362.

[47] Stiglitz, J.E., Sen, A., & Fitoussi, J.-P. (2001). Measurement of economic performance and social progress. http://www.stiglitz-sen-fitoussi.fr/documents/rapport_anglais.pdf

[48] Canadian Index of Wellbeing. (2014). How are Ontarians really doing? A Provincial report on Ontario wellbeing. Waterloo, ON: Canadian Index of Wellbeing and University of Waterloo.

[49] Muhamma, E. (2006). Sustainable Tourism Development and Environmental Management for Developing Countries. *Problems and perspectives in Management*, 4(2), 14-30.

[50] Mirsanjari, M. M., Ildoromi, A., & Yavarzadeh, M. (2012). Sustainability and its role in environmental ecotourism management. *Pollution Research*, 31(1), 117-120.

[51] Jamal, T., Borges, M., & Stronza, A. (2006). The institutionalisation of ecotourism: Certification, cultural equity and praxis. *Journal of Ecotourism*, 5(3), 145-175.

[52] Dawson, J., Johnston, M. J., Stewart, E.J., Lemieux, C.J., Lemelin, R. H., Maher, P. T., & Grimwood, B. S. R. (2011). Ethical considerations of last chance tourism. *Journal of Ecotourism*, 10(3), 250-265.

[53] Grimwood, B. S. R., Yudina, O., Muldoon, M., & Qiu, J. (2015). Responsibility in tourism: A discursive analysis. *Annals of Tourism Research*, 50, 22-38.

[54] Cohen, S.A., Higham, J.E.S., Peeters, P. & Gössling, S. Understanding and governing sustainable tourism mobility: Psychological and behavioural approaches. Oxon/New York: Routledge; 2014

[55] Phillip, S., Hunter, C., & Blackstock, K, (2010). A tipology for defining agritourism. *Tourism Management*, 31, 754-758.

[56] Flanigan, S., Blackstock, K., & Hunter, C. (2014). Agritourism from the perspective of providers and visitors: a typology-based study. *Tourism Management*, 40, 394-405.

[57] Delgado, R., Sánchez-Marañón, M., Martín-García, J. M., Aranda, V., Serrano-Bernardo, F., & Rosúa, J. L. (2007). Impact of ski pistes on soil properties: a case study from a mountainous area in the Mediterranean region. *Soil Use and Management*, 2007, 23, 269-277.

[58] Serrano-Bernardo, F.A., & Rosúa-Campos, J. L. (2008). Seedling establishment of two shrubby plants native to the Sierra Nevada mountain range. *Central European Journal of Biology*, 3(4), 451-460.

[59] Butler, R. W. (1980). The concept of a tourist area cycle of evolution: Implications for management of resources. *The Canadian Geographer*, 24(1): 5-12.

[60] UNWTO (United Nations World Tourism Organization) (1981), Saturation of Tourist Destinations, *Report of the Secretary General*, Madrid.

[61] Butler, R. W. (1991). Tourism, environment, and sustainable development. *Environmental Conservation*, 18(3), 201-209.

[62] Agarwal, S. (1997). The resort cycle and seaside tourism: an assessment of its applicability and validity. *Tourism Management*, 18(2), 65-73.

[63] Agarwal, S. (2002). Restructuring seaside tourism. The resort lifecycle. *Annals of Tourism Research*, 29(1), 25-55.

[64] Weaver, D. B. (2012). Organic, incremental and induced paths to sustainable mass tourism convergence. *Tourism Management*, 33, 1030-1037.

[65] Kelly, J., Haider, W., & Williams, P. W. (2007). A behavioral assessment of tourism transportation options for reducing energy consumption and greenhouse gases. *Journal of Travel Research*, 45(3), 297-309.

[66] Filimonau, V., Dickinson, J. E., Robbins, D., & Reddy, M. V. (2011) A critical review of methods for tourism climate change appraisal: life cycle assessment as a new approach. *Journal of Sustainable Tourism*, 19(3), 301-324.

[67] Filimonau, V., Dickinson, J., Robbins, D., & Reddy, M. V. (2013). The role of „indirect" greenhouse gas emissions in tourism: Assessing the hidden carbon impacts from a holiday package tour. *Transportation Research Part A, 54*, 78-91.

[68] UNEP/UNWTO (United Nations Environment Programme and World Tourism Organization) (2012). Tourism in the Green Economy-Background report. UNEP/UNWTO: Madrid.

[69] Chavez-Baeza, C., & Sheinbaum-Pardo, C. (2014). Sustainable passenger road transport scenarios to reduce fuel consumption, air pollutants and GHG (greenhouse gas) emissions in the Mexico City Metropolitan Area. *Energy, 66*, 624-634.

[70] Takeshita, T. (2011). Global scenarios of air pollutant emissions from road transport through to 2050. *International Journal of Environmental Research and Public Health, 8*, 3032-3062.

[71] Morrell, P. (2007). An evaluation of possible EU air transport emissions trading scheme allocation methods. *Energy Policy, 35*, 5562-5570.

[72] Howitt, O., J. A., Revol, V. G. N., Smith, I. J., & Rodger, C. J. (2010). Carbon emissions from international cruise ship passengers" travel to and from New Zealand. *Energy Policy, 38*, 2552-2560.

[73] Saboori, B., Sapri, M., & bin Baba, M. (2014) Economic growth, energy consumption and CO_2 emissions in OECD (Organization for Economic Co-operation and Development)"s transport sector: A fully modified bi-directional relationship approach. *Energy, 66*, 150-161.

[74] Tang, Z., Shang, J., Shi, C., Liu, Z., Bi, K. (2014). Decoupling indicators of CO_2 emissions from the tourism industry in China: 1990–2012. *Ecological Indicators, 46*, 390-397.

[75] Chapman, L. (2007). Transport and climate change: a review. *Journal of Transport Geography, 15*, 354-367.

[76] Marsden, G., & Rye, T. (2010). The governance of transport and climate change. *Journal of Transport Geography, 18*, 669-678.

[77] Tight, M. R., Bristow, A. L., Pridmore, A., & May, A. D. (2005). What is a sustainable level of CO_2 emissions from transport activity in the UK in 2050? *Transport Policy, 12*, 235-244.

In: Ecotourism
Editor: Shannon C. Brophy

ISBN: 978-1-63482-027-1
© 2015 Nova Science Publishers, Inc.

Chapter 2

ISLAND ECOTOURISM IN BRUNEI DARUSSALAM: ITS ROLE IN BIODIVERSITY CONSERVATION AND ENVIRONMENTAL EDUCATION

Azman Ahmad and Alifatul Haziqah Abu Hanipah*
Universiti Brunei Darussalam, Brunei

ABSTRACT

Islands are among the most visited tourist destinations in the world. They are exposed to all kinds of risks with often inadequate resources and fragile ecosystems. The prospect of ecotourism development in tropical islands are enormous, since most islands host distinctive flora and fauna with some endemic species, colourful coral reefs and marine ecosystems, as well as unique environmental features and appealing land- and seascapes. Brunei Darussalam has 33 islands spread across its shores, which are largely uninhabited. Among them is Selirong Island, an island dominantly covered by mangrove forests, which has been developed as an ecotourism destination. This chapter begins with a historical overview of the development of Selirong Island as a forest production site and now as an ecotourism attraction, and later examines how interpretation can be used as a tool for the conservation and preservation of its rich

* azman.ahmad@ubd.edu.bn.

biodiversity, as well as for the environmental education of tourists and visitors to the island.

INTRODUCTION

As a new player to the tourism sector, Brunei Darussalam manages to capture a slight but growing percentage of the global tourism market. Brunei Darussalam carves the smallest slice of tourism pie received in Southeast Asia with only 0.23% of total tourist arrivals in the region in 2012 (World Travel and Tourism Council, 2014). Tourist arrivals in the country account for 224,904 tourists in 2013, with an average of 185,513 annually over the last ten years (Tourism Development Department, 2014). Brunei Darussalam is not particularly well-known among tourists as a potential destination, compared to other neighbouring countries such as Malaysia, Indonesia, Singapore or Thailand. Tourism development has been progressing rather slowly in Brunei Darussalam, even though it has already established some of the support facilities and services necessary for tourism, such as accommodation, banking, communications, transport, and visitor attractions.

Ecotourism has been singled out as one of the tourism products that has the potential to be developed in Brunei Darussalam. The country"s long-term development plan listed several projects to further develop its tourism-related infrastructure, which include the developments of Ulu Temburong National Park, ecotourism destinations, forest recreational parks and marine parks (Government of Brunei Darussalam, 2007). A new tourism master plan designed to steer the country"s tourism direction for the period 2011 to 2015 explicitly declared natural assets as one of the clusters it will be focusing on. The Ministry of Industry and Primary Resources, which is responsible for tourism policy and development in Brunei Darussalam, is working closely with relevant stakeholders in the private sector in producing ecotourism packages and promoting the country as an ecotourism destination (Too, 2014). With 78% of the country"s 5,769 square kilometres of land still covered in primary forest, and 55% of the total land area being dedicated as forest reserves and permanent forest estates under its National Forestry Policy (Thien, 2010), Brunei Darussalam has interesting and unique natural areas that can be offered as ecotourism sites.

As a coastal nation, Brunei Darussalam owns 33 islands altogether, most of which are located in the inner Brunei Bay or major rivers, whilst only two of them are found offshore. Only three of these islands are inhabited and the remaining majority are still unspoiled. The uninhabited islands are covered with pristine primary forest, although several areas have been cleared for agriculture. Most of the islands support few flora and fauna, but some have become homes to endangered species (Agbayani et al., 1992).

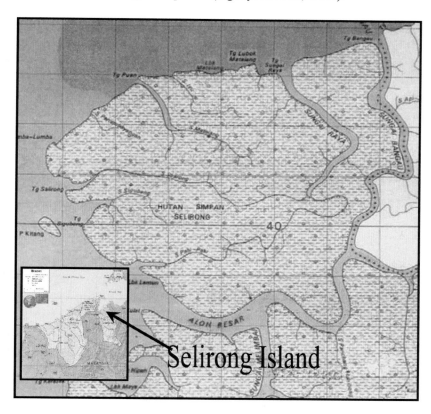

Figure 1. Selirong Island (Inset: Location of Selirong Island in Brunei).

Selirong Island or *Pulau Selirong* is one of the uninhabited islands located in the Brunei Bay on the northern end of the Temburong District (refer to Figure 1). In the local language, *Pulau Selirong* literally means „Mosquito Island". Selirong Island was gazetted as a Forest Reserve in 1948 (Gazette Notification 99/1948) under the Forest Act of 1934. Selirong Island is now classified as a Forest Recreational Park, as it has the potential for ecotourism and for recreational, educational and research purposes. The island has a total area of 2,566 hectares, with approximately 2,409 hectares or 94% of the surface area covered in mangrove forests, whilst the remaining 157 hectares are water areas (Zamora, 1987). It is estimated that 18,418 hectares or 3.2% of the country's total land surface is made up of mangrove forests (Anderson & Marsden, 1984). Thus, Selirong Island accounts for approximately 13% of the Brunei Darussalam's mangrove forests.

The mangrove forests in Selirong Island are dominated by *Rhizophora apiculata* (a common mangrove species) or *Bakau* trees, which normally grow up to 7 metres in height and 10 centimetres in diameter. However, in Selirong Island these mangrove trees have grown to reach greater heights of 30 metres and diameter of 60 centimetres (Kashio, 2002). The colossal character of the island's mangrove trees is attributed to the conservation initiatives and policy implemented by the government at Selirong Island, as well as other forest reserves in the country. As such, the pristine mangrove ecosystem in Selirong Island is understood to be exceptional in this part of the world (Kashio, 2002). Therefore, Brunei Darussalam can be said to possess the best preserved mangrove forests in the region, which can provide a platform to offer them and Selirong Island as a distinctive ecotourism destination.

HISTORICAL USE OF MANGROVES

The mangrove forests play an important part of the traditional life of the population in the country. In the past, Brunei Darussalam's mangroves were a major source of wood for the charcoal industry. The *Bakau* trees also yield cutch - a dye extract used in tanning leather and caulking boats. The wood chips were utilised in making textile, paper and the very popular food flavouring, monosodium glutamate. Mangrove charcoal is also traditionally used by Brunei women for post-natal treatment. The local women believe that after giving birth, a mother should stay near the charcoal fire to warm herself, as the heat accordingly helps to contract the muscles of the womb. The fuelwood was likewise used for ironing and daily cooking.

The Forestry Department under the Ministry of Industry and Primary Resources is authorised to manage Selirong Island. To a greater extent, the Forestry Department controlled the activities carried out in forest reserves. In the case of Selirong Island, a Mangrove Working Circle Plan was introduced for the period 1958 to 1967, which also covered the Labu Forest Reserve, an area located on the north of Temburong District, adjacent to Selirong Island. The detailed working plan prescribed the areas that were to be felled each year, and the methods to be adopted in growing new crops (Government of Brunei Darussalam, 1958).

It was reported that some adjustments to the Working Circle Plan were made in the mid-1960s, particularly for the use of the mangrove products. Originally, it was drafted in the plan that the mangrove trees were required for firewood. In 1966, it was identified that the mangrove forests were demanded for piling poles and charcoal. With the large amount of new building undertaken in towns throughout the country, this generated a heavy demand for *Bakau* piling posts. It was also realised that the mangrove forests needed to be carefully managed, in view of the increasing pressure on them owing to the recently aroused interest in mangrove chips for rayon fibre and charcoal for export (Government of Brunei Darussalam, 1966).

Overall, the 1958-1967 Working Plan for the mangrove forests of Selirong Island had been adhered to. In 1967, a survey was conducted in the areas declared to be worked out, and as suspected, it was found that exploitation had followed the waterways without any real depth of penetration. The plan was closely monitored to ensure permit holders were to adopt some means of mechanical extraction in order to fully exploit the areas (Government of Brunei Darussalam, 1967).

According to the Forestry Department, seven compartments of Selirong Island had so far been given concession for felling, dating as far back as 1962 and as recent as 1996. As a type of forest management approach, clear felling normally involves the practice of completely felling and removing a stand of trees, which is quickly followed by the replanting of the cleared area. At Selirong Island, clear felling was adopted in three compartments. In some of the compartments designated for felling at Selirong Island, the practice of selective felling was also involved. It has been observed that rapid regeneration has since taken place in all these compartments, producing dense and young population of *Rhizophora* trees. Today, logging in Selirong Island is not permitted to complement its protected area status.

Tourism Development at Selirong Island

Since the designation of Selirong Island as a Forest Recreational Park, the Forestry Department has undertaken several initiatives to develop the island as an ecotourism and recreational site. In 1994, they built a 2 kilometre-long elevated boardwalk from Mataing River to Palu-Palu River. The walkway enables visitors to walk through the park and observe the enormous mangrove trees with overgrown roots.

In 1999, a guard house was constructed at the park to assist visitors entering the island. The guard house which serves as a control post is located at Tanjung Puan at the mouth of the Mataing River. Visitors to the park have to register at the guard house, before they are allowed to proceed with their tour around the island. Every group of visitor to the park will be escorted by a ranger from the Forestry Department and an armed officer throughout the visit. This is to ensure the safety and security of every visitor to the island as it is in close proximity to the border of Sarawak, Malaysia.

There are several visitor facilities built at the park, including an observation tower located along Selirong River in the mid-section of the boardwalk, as well as resting huts along the route of the boardwalk. These facilities provide convenience for visitors to break their tour of the island and enjoy the sights and sounds of the mangrove atmosphere. There is no on-site tourist accommodation built at the park, because of the relatively small area, remote location, and the need to minimise development within the fragile environment. There are also interpretive signs posted along the elevated boardwalk to inform visitors of the distinctive flora and fauna and to educate visitors on the growth process of the mangrove trees at the park. These interpretive signs form a crucial component of ecotourism, whereby tourists are able to learn and understand the unique features found at the island. The Forestry Department further plans to develop the country's first mangrove centre, consisting of research laboratories and interpretive facilities at Selirong Island (Masli, 2010). This would enable students and scientists to carry out research and education on the mangrove environment, as well as tourists to learn more about the wetlands ecosystem.

Travelling to Selirong Island can be arranged through charter tours by means of commercial motorised boats. These tours normally include boat transfer, box lunch and an experienced wildlife guide. Other options for visitors would be to hire water taxis from the city which will take them to the island. The direct trip takes approximately 45 minutes, but can be much shorter during high tide.

The tourism infrastructure developed and planned for Selirong Island complements the wealth of biodiversity, wildlife and vegetation found at the park, which makes the island suitable to be promoted as an ecotourism destination. The island is appropriate for day visitors, as well as nature-lovers, ecotourists, wildlife researchers and students. The island's environment is a nursery for a variety of aquatic organisms such as fish, crabs, shrimps, prawns, cockles and barnacles, as well as shore and water birds such as storks, egrets, plovers, herons, kingfishers, sandpipers, terns, redshanks and hornbills. There are about 40 species of birds and various species of reptiles and fishes inhabiting Selirong Island, including estuarine snakes, green turtles, estuarine crocodiles, mud skippers and monitor lizards (Charles, 2002). The island is also home to interesting mammals including proboscis monkeys, crab-eating macaques, slivered langurs, flying foxes, fruit bats, flying lemurs (colugos), plantain squirrels and small-clawed otters. Proboscis monkeys are endemic to the island of Borneo, and there are several populations of these primates in Selirong Island. Flying lemurs or colugos are uncommon in a mangrove forest (Charles, 2002), and hence their presence in the mangrove island place Selirong Island in an exceptional and potential position as an ecotourism site. This is coupled by the fact that the island's undisturbed mangrove trees have been well-preserved and developed unusually larger than those found elsewhere.

Aside from the wealth of biodiversity in the park, visitors to Selirong Island will also appreciate the local community that reside in the surrounding waterways. On route to Selirong Island, visitors will observe socio-economic marine activities, particularly small-scale traditional and artisanal fishermen harvesting their catch around the island. Brunei Bay and the estuaries provide the core fishing ground in the country for artisanal fishermen who use traditional gears such as tidal funnel bag net, simple bottom set gillnet, cast net, drifting gillnet, fish trap, crab trap and palisade trap for their daily fishing activities. It is, however, disturbing to note that this fishing ground also attracts fishermen from Sarawak, Malaysia, and there could possibly be illegal fishing carried out in Brunei Darussalam's side of the border (Ibrahim, 2002). If left unchecked, this could create a potential conflict between the two countries, and a detriment to the mangrove ecosystem of the Selirong Island.

Visitor statistics at Selirong Island has been fluctuating over the years from 1996 to 2014 (refer to Figure 2). Tourist number has been significantly reduced particularly from 1997, because the Forestry Department has curbed the visitor intensity to the park in order to minimise the negative impacts generated by the visitors. It is estimated that the maximum number of persons permissible at the park is 640 persons or visits per day (Ahmad, 2002). Based on the visitor statistics, it can be deduced that current visitation to Selirong Island is well under the carrying capacity of the park. For example, the year 2011 has received among the highest number of visitors over the period, reaching 962 people, which therefore amounts to only about 2.6 visitors per day. From these data, it can be concluded that current visitation trends to Selirong Island have not exceeded the capacity of the park. Due to the low visitation, it can also be inferred that tourism has not presented much adverse impacts on the physical environment of the island.

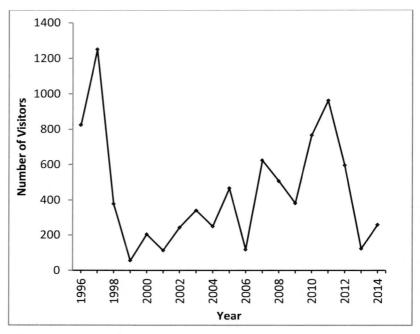

Figure 2. Visitor statistics at Selirong Island (2014 data until October 2014 only).

CONSERVATION AND EDUCATION THROUGH ECOTOURISM

By 2020, The World Tourism Organisation (WTO) predicts that there will be 1.6 billion international tourist arrivals and tourism receipts will reach US$2,000 billion globally. Nature tourism is estimated to generate 7% of all international travel expenditure (Ceballos-Lascuráin, 1996). In general, tourism has been growing at 4% annually, whereas nature travel has been increasing between 10% and 30% annually (Reingold, 1993). Similarly, WTO (1998) indicates that ecotourism and all nature-related forms of tourism account for approximately 20% of total international travel. These statistics demonstrate that the ecotourism sector is progressing fast and it is becoming a significant activity that contributes substantially to the world's economy and to global travel and tourism industry.

Ceballos-Lascuráin defines ecotourism as "travelling to relatively undisturbed natural areas with the objective of admiring, studying, and enjoying the scenery and its wild plants and animals, as well as any cultural features found there" (1991, p. 31). The International Ecotourism Society's definition of ecotourism is responsible travel to natural areas that conserves the environment and improves the well-being of local people (Lindberg & Hawkins, 1993). Weaver (2005) further identifies three components that differentiate ecotourism with other nature-based tourism products and attractions, namely the inclusion of culture in the natural areas, provision of learning opportunities and experiences, and sustainable planning and management of the ecotourism products.

The provision of learning opportunities and experiences can be obtained from interpretation that is available either inside or outside of the natural areas visited. Weiler and Davis define interpretation as "an educational, illustrative and entertaining activity which aims at providing the visitor with an insight into the interrelationships of the various resources and systems comprising the natural environment by first-hand experiences" (1993, p. 93). On-site interpretation can be in static form such as interpretation centres, and self-guided walks using information signs or displays, or it can also be personalised through guides providing information. Off-site interpretation can come in the forms of guidebooks, photographs, internet, promotional videos, virtual reality, or word of mouth. Interpretation in ecotourism is equivalent to, or often interchangeably known as, environmental education which serves to provide learnings about species and the associated ecology of an area, and learnings about the sensitive nature of environmental areas and how to minimise tourist and other impacts. It also involves learning about the local community, its socio-economy and culture. In other words, interpretation can provide learning opportunities and understanding about the natural as well as cultural attractions of the area visited.

Orams writes that "an effective interpretation programme may be a means by which nature-based tourism can truly become ,ecotourism'" (1996, p. 92). An interpretation programme can only be effective if it is able to change visitors" knowledge of the natural area, and affect their attitudes and values towards the environment, leading towards a greater appreciation of the natural environment and a positive influence in their behaviour (Madin & Fenton, 2004).

Figure 3. Interpretive Leaflets on Selirong Island.

At Selirong Island, interpretation or environmental education is provided both on-site and off-site. On-site interpretation at the park includes brochures, display boards, briefings by park rangers and information signs. The Forestry Department, with the support of Universiti Brunei Darussalam and Ramsar Centre of Japan, has produced brochures for visitors containing information on Selirong Island and its wildlife, including the flying lemurs or colugos, as the island's primary attraction (refer to Figure 3). The brochure on the colugos features important facts about the behaviour or characteristic of a colugo, in terms of where it can be found, what it eats, or how to distinguish it from a flying squirrel. Such brochures serve to educate tourists and visitors about the wildlife species and the mangrove ecology of Selirong Island. Apart from imparting knowledge onto visitors about the island's rich biodiversity, the Forestry Department also produces brochures that inform visitors on the importance of conserving wildlife and remind them of the various offences that breach wildlife protection laws with the aim of averting destruction on the wildlife and the island environment (Ibrahim & Ahmad, 2002).

There are display boards erected at the guard house, which also present information on the wildlife found at the park, including those on the various mammals such as the flying fox, flying lemur or colugo, and long-tailed macaque (refer to Figure 4). The unusual root system of the mangrove trees which comes in several forms including knee, creeping, stilts, plank, respiratory and aerial roots, are also shown in one of the display boards. This highlights the rare and resourceful ways of natural adaptation developed by the mangrove trees in the island. The display boards are informative and contain useful material for visitors to understand the mangrove ecosystem in the island. The Forestry Department used stainless steel for the display boards, which made them resilient against the humid condition of the island.

Figure 4. A Display Board on Mammals at Selirong Island.

Figure 5. A Tree Label at Selirong Island.

Figure 6. Visitor Briefing by Forestry Rangers at Selirong Island.

Along the elevated boardwalk, there are signs or labels placed on trees to inform visitors of the local and scientific name of the trees (refer to Figure 5). These tree labels are simple, yet they are helpful to tell visitors of the diverse mangrove trees that inhabit the island. The role of this interpretation is to enable visitors to learn the local language and stimulate interest on the medicinal property and local use of the various tree species, which are normally shared by the park rangers who accompany the visitors.

An on-site interpretation is also provided to visitors through briefings by park rangers. Upon arrival at the guard house, all visitors would receive an explanatory session on the history and background of the park and Selirong Island (refer to Figure 6). The session would normally include an introduction to the flora and fauna of the island as well as the unique features that can be found at the park. Following the introductory briefing, the park rangers would accompany the visitors throughout their tour around the island, and share vital and specific information about the wildlife species available.

EVALUATION OF INTERPRETATION PROGRAMME AT SELIRONG ISLAND

To date, no survey among visitors of Selirong Island has been conducted to evaluate the interpretation provided at the park. Hence, in order to gauge the effectiveness of interpretation at Selirong Island in delivering environmental education as well as providing an enjoyable and meaningful experience to the visitor, a survey was carried out among visitors to the island. The survey serves to examine visitor satisfaction and experience with the interpretation variables including both on-site (display boards, leaflets and guides) and off-site interpretation (guidebook, internet, tourism agency, media, and friends and relatives). The outcome of the survey provides useful insights on the level of effectiveness of delivery of the conservation messages through interpretation provided at Selirong Island. The survey focuses on assessing the relationship between satisfaction of visitors with interpretation and its ability to affect visitor values to the environment.

METHODOLOGY

A small survey was carried out over a brief period between October to November 2014. The survey questionnaire was comprised of two main parts, the first of which collects information on visitor profiles, including gender, age, place of residence, education, employment, membership to environmental, conservation or outdoor organisation, number of park visit, and sources of pre-visit information. The second section of the survey examines the tourists" experience of visiting the island. This includes questions on the levels of visitor satisfaction with each interpretation product (display boards, leaflets and guides or staff), reasons for visiting the island, and the extent to which the interpretation stimulated visitors to think about issues presented and develop deeper meaningful connections with the island.

The survey questionnaires were distributed to visitors of Selirong Island, through the assistance of the Forestry Department. The survey questionnaires were handed out by staff of the Forestry Department to visitors at the end of their visit, and to be returned immediately after the survey was completed. As a result of the lack of return of the survey through this approach, a different method was adopted. The latter involves creating an online survey via Survey Monkey, and distributing the survey questionnaire online to a targeted group of visitors to Selirong Island. This group of visitors was searched through social networks and websites including Facebook, Twitter, Instagram, Pinterest, Tumblr, 500px, Flickr, Tripadvisor and Wanderlust, based on their posts of visits to Selirong Island. As a result, a greater number of respondents was obtained from the online survey. The survey only considers respondents who made their visits to Selirong Island from 2007 onward, in order to reduce the dissimilarity with the interpretation settings at the Selirong Island between different years.

The data collected through the surveys were then coded for entry into the Statistical Package for Social Sciences (SPSS). Methods of analysis employed to interpret the data include descriptive statistics, frequencies and cross-tabulations.

RESULTS

During the survey period, Selirong Island received a very low visitor count. This explains the lack of return of completed survey questionnaires from visitors that were distributed through the Forestry Department. As shown in Figure 2, the number of visitors to Selirong Island for the year 2014 is 257 with only one visitor in October, which indicates the low visitation, and thus, the difficulty in getting a high response rate. The online survey approach has collected data from 24 respondents, and the results presented in this chapter are obtained from this small sample.

The survey received an equal number of female and male respondents. The most common age group recorded is the 25-34 years age group (50%). There is also quite a high number of respondents aged between 15 and 24 years (33%). The majority of the respondents reside in Brunei Darussalam (88%), with 63% of them coming from Brunei-Muara district while the rest are from Tutong (13%), Kuala Belait (8%) and Temburong (4%). Respondents residing overseas only account for 13%, mainly from the United Kingdom and France.

In terms of the respondents" level of education, 42% and 38% of them obtained a bachelor degree/diploma and a postgraduate qualification, respectively, as being their highest level of education. Only few respondents have completed technical (13%) and secondary schooling (8%). More than half (54%) of the respondents are currently employed in full-time work and 21% are students.

With regard to their membership to environmental, conservation or outdoor recreation group, only 33% of the respondents said that they belong to one, which varied from Brunei Nature Society, BruWILD and National Youth Volunteers. In addition, most of the respondents (71%) indicated that it was their first time visiting Selirong Island. However, 67% of the respondents have visited other recreational parks less than six times in the past year. Although a substantial proportion of the respondents are first-time visitors to Selirong Island, they are regular visitors to protected areas or nature-based areas in the country.

An analysis of the pre-visit information reveals that 46% of the respondents obtained information about Selirong Island from friends and relatives, which is the highest among other sources (refer to Table 1). This is followed by Brunei Forestry Department website (25%), Selirong Island brochure and guidebook (13%), and internet site (13%). None of the visitors surveyed used other media such as radio, television, newspaper and magazine as well as tourism travel agency or company. Interestingly, 25% of the respondents visited Selirong Island without obtaining any prior information about the destination.

Table 1. Sources of Information on Selirong Island

Sources	Percentage of Respondents
Friends/relatives	46
Brunei Forestry Department website	25
Selirong Island brochure/guidebook	13
Internet site	13
Radio/TV/newspaper/magazine	-
Tourism travel agency/company	-
Did not obtain any information	25

Using cross-tabulation analysis between age, level of education and source of information, it was found that sources via friends and relatives as well as Brunei Forestry Department website are mostly preferred by respondents aged between 25 and 34 years (64% and 67% respectively) who had obtained higher level of education including bachelor degree/diploma (46% and 33% respectively) and a postgraduate qualification (36% and 67% respectively). On the other hand, younger respondents (aged between 15 to 24 years) tend to visit the island without seeking any pre-visit information (50%). The latter finding is not surprising since the younger respondents went to Selirong Island as part of their educational field trip planned by their schools, and could not bother to find information from other sources (as shown in Table 1), aside from their teachers. The survey also received comments from respondents on the quality of the information on Selirong Island. Some of the positive comments reflect visitors" satisfaction with the quality of conveyed information and expressed it as good and useful. On the other hand, negative comments received from visitors mainly focused on the limited information about the island, and lack of marketing and promotion of the island. Some respondents also highlighted the lack of availability of printed information and insignificant internet information about the island. The island was not well-advertised, and hence not all respondents realise its existence.

In order to identify visitor motivations for visiting the island, survey respondents were asked to rate a list of reasons according to how important they were for them to visit.

Table 2. Reasons for Visiting Selirong Island (Percentage)

Reasons	Level of Importance				
	Not Important	Of Little Importance	Somewhat Important	Very Important	Extremely Important
Rest and relax	4	9	43	30	14
See the sights	-	17	22	35	26
Be with family or friend	5	18	27	36	14
Close to nature and enjoy nature	-	4	26	44	26
Physically active	9	13	30	26	22
Engage in recreational activities	-	4	22	39	35
Learn about native plants and animals	-	13	22	43	22
Alone	40	30	17	4	9

As can be seen from Table 2, more than 40% of the visitors considered it as very important and somewhat important to be close to nature and enjoy nature, to learn about the native plants and animals, and to rest and relax. This is followed by the need to engage in recreational activities (39%), and to see the sights (35%) and to be with family and friends (36%), while the least important reason to visit the island is to be alone. Some visitors commented specific reasons for visiting Selirong Island, including photo outing organised by photographic club, industrial university placement and university field trip. Visitors also highlighted that they were anticipating to be involved in organised environmentally-related physical activities rather than merely walking along the walkways, but there were none offered when they visited the island.

The survey also elicited visitors" level of satisfaction on the various interpretation variables provided at Selirong Island, namely display boards, leaflets or brochures, and guide services (refer to Table 3). Interpretation through the display boards, in terms of use, size and information conveyed, received the highest percentage (37%-38%) of satisfied responses. It is also observed that there is a relatively high proportion (33%) of respondents that are neither satisfied nor dissatisfied with the display boards. Similar responses are also obtained for other interpretation, namely leaflets (33%) and information on the leaflets (37%), as well as for assistance from guides and staff (35%).

An analysis of the performance of different market segments (age, education level and frequency of visit) with satisfaction scores for interpretation variables generates an interesting result. The majority of the respondents who are satisfied with the display boards at Selirong Island are those who had obtained degree or diploma (>22%) and postgraduate (44%) qualifications, aged between 25 and 34 years (>56%) and were first-time visitors (>50%). More than 60% of those who are neither satisfied nor dissatisfied with the leaflets or brochures on Selirong Island are those aged between 25 and 34 years, with a degree or diploma qualification (>40%) and were first-time visitors (>57%) to the island.

When further asked whether the visitors felt that the interpretive experience stimulated them to think and develop connections with Selirong Island, it was found that they are likely to have been provoked by the interpretation to think about the issues being presented and potentially make lasting connections. More than half of the visitors agreed that the interpretive experience made them think (58%), want to know more (63%) and/or intrigued them (54%). However, many visitors also felt rather neutral when asked whether the interpretive experience made them curious (54%) and talk about what they heard (50%).

Table 3. Visitors' Satisfaction with Interpretation Programmes at Selirong Island (Percentage)

Types of Interpretation	Level of Satisfaction					
	Very Dissatisfied	Dissatisfied	Neither	Satisfied	Very Satisfied	Not Applicable
Use of display boards	-	21	33	38	8	-
Size of display boards	-	13	33	37	13	4
Information on display boards	-	13	33	37	13	4
Leaflets	-	17	33	13	8	29
Information on leaflets	-	13	37	13	8	29
Assistance from guides/staffs	4	9	35	22	13	17

DISCUSSION

The market segment identified comprises of equal amount of male and female, mainly aged below 35, well-educated and have higher status occupations compared to the general population. The findings on the Selirong Island market segment are similar with other surveys carried out in other international parks such as those found by Griffin and Archer (2001), Wearing et al. (2008) and Kaltenborn et al. (2011). Although, a small sample is captured in this chapter, it is an important indicator that Selirong Island is recognised as a place to visit for ecotourism and recreational activity. The main recorded reason for making a trip to Selirong Island is to be close to nature and learn about the native flora and fauna. Selirong Island is well-known for its pristine mangrove ecosystems and a home to a diverse array of wildlife. The respondents in the survey confirm this impression placing a very high emphasis on enjoying nature and learning about the native wildlife. Many visitors also placed importance on relaxation and rest as their purpose of visiting Selirong Island. Its relative isolation makes Selirong Island an ideal destination for those who wish to be away from civilisation and enjoy a moment of peace and tranquil amidst nature.

However, its isolation and remoteness also gives Selirong Island anonymity, and thereby lack of information and visitation. Hence, the survey conducted among visitors to the island only managed to capture a small sample. Selirong Island is not a common place to visit. It is notable that Selirong Island is not highly promoted or publicised to the general public. Finding information about the island in preparation for visit is problematic as expressed by the respondents. Many found that printed information about the island is rare and information on the internet is limited. Instead, Selirong Island is widely exposed through friends and relatives as discovered in the survey. This indicates the importance of word of mouth to publicise Selirong Island as an ecotourism and recreational destination. Beside friends and relatives, the next preferred source is Brunei Forestry Department website. Most of the respondents who sought information about the island prior to their visit are those who aged between 25 and 34 years, and had obtained either a degree, diploma or postgraduate qualification. This indicates that these market segments tend to make a research and learn more about the island in preparation for their visit.

Visitors who participated in the survey expressed a mixed response on the level of satisfaction with the interpretation variables including display boards, leaflets and assistance from guides and staffs at Selirong Island. Among all the variables, a high degree of satisfaction is rated for display boards. Many are satisfied with the use of display boards, the size of the displays and the information contained in the boards. On the other hand, leaflets and guides did not have any implication to the visitors, as these variables are mostly rated as neither satisfied nor dissatisfied. The findings suggest that visitors aged between 25 and 34 years, had higher qualifications and were first-time visitor, tend to be satisfied with the display boards but felt neither satisfied nor dissatisfied with the leaflets and guides. Based on these findings, it is concluded that display boards are more preferred interpretation for visitors to extract information compared to leaflets and guides. A similar survey conducted by Ahmad (2008) revealed similar findings where 69% of the park visitors in Brunei Darussalam used information signs or displays, 15% employed guide services, 11% made use of the interpretation centre, and only 6% drew from park guidebooks and brochures. This indicates the popularity of information signs or display boards as a tool to educate visitors about the natural and cultural environment at a park.

Surprisingly, some quoted that leaflets and guides are not applicable at Selirong Island. This could be explained by the absence of printed leaflets and the lack of experienced guides to assist visitors to learn about the island.

Ahmad (2015) writes that guides or staff at the island gave very little information or advice to visitors at Selirong Island. They did not possess inherent knowledge about the wildlife species found in the park and, they also appeared to be lacking in interest in appreciating the mangrove environment and its wildlife (Ahmad, 2015). The uneven level of satisfaction with the interpretation at Selirong Island revealed in the survey may suggest a low quality experience for most of the visitors. This is unfortunate for both visitors and park managers as the opportunity to have an enjoyable learning experience and disseminate environmental conservation messages can be hampered through low impact interpretation at Selirong Island. The survey conducted by Ahmad (2008), which ascertains that 89% of park users suggest for more environmental education programmes to be provided at the protected areas, implies that visitors to natural areas are interested in the conservation aspects of the parks. Selirong Island should take the opportunity to improve its interpretation programmes and ensure its effectiveness in providing environmental education to visitors. Park managers need to review and upgrade the interpretation programmes, which may include the provision of adequate number of informative leaflets and trained guides and staffs. In a study done by Walker and Moscardo (2014), it was highlighted that staff expertise and staff dedication, the ability of staff to provide security, to assist people to make personal connections and to elicit participant trust is important for most of the cruise passengers. Guides can potentially exert more influence on the visitors as they can incorporate active delivery of messages with a multi-sensory, complex social interaction when communicating with visitors (Hughes and Morrison-Saunders, 2005; Munro et al., 2008). Previous research also suggested that successful interpretation encourages positive conservation attitudes among visitors (Jacobs and Harms, 2014; Walker and Moscardo, 2014).

Ham (2007) advocates that there is a link between interpretation and behavioural influence based on the extent to which visitors identify with the interpretation material and how they are provoked to think along the themes presented, which in turn may influence beliefs, attitudes and ultimately, behaviour. From the survey conducted among visitors of Selirong Island, this chapter found that over half of the visitors are likely to have been provoked by the interpretation to think about the issues being presented, and the experience made them want to know more and fascinated them. However, it is worth noting that over half of the visitors felt rather neutral that the experience made them curious and talk to others about what they learnt or heard during the visit. It would appear that, based on these findings, current provisions of interpretation did not necessarily have a strong impact to the visitors. As suggested before, park managers may need to revise their strategy in providing an effective interpretation featuring a strong conservational theme. Ham (2007) finds that interpretation with compelling presentations of strong and relevant themes would stand the greatest chance of having enduring impacts on their audiences.

Further research is needed in terms of robust studies to facilitate the development of a clear understanding of interpretation programmes" influence on visitor behaviour in Selirong Island as well as other protected areas and ecotourism destinations in Brunei Darussalam. There are several limitations with this chapter that would need to be addressed if this area was to be further researched. It was uncertain that interpretive variables affect visitor's environmental values and attitude since the survey only focused on one experimental group. Future research should employ control and experimental groups in order to evaluate interpretive influences on visitors. Assuming other variables are not significantly different and the two groups differ primarily in exposure to interpretation, the impact of the interpretive variables can be assessed by comparing the findings between the control and experimental group (Munro et al., 2008; Jacobs and Harms, 2014). Other important factors to ensure the validity of the research include adequate sample size as well as post-experience follow up. Sample size must be adequate and statistically valid and this can be achieved through a longer time frame survey. Post-interpretive experience follow ups as recommended by Munro et al. (2008) are to determine if any changes in knowledge, attitudes or behaviour recorded immediately after the experience are transient or more permanent.

CONCLUSION

Isolation is often considered a drawback to those trading products around the globe, but for tourism, it may be a benefit in that it tends to make the destination more attractive and exotic, especially in the case of small islands. In addition, d'Hauteserre writes that "islands are the second most important holiday destination after the category of historic cities" (2003, p.49).

In the ecotourism context, education and interpretation can serve two different roles, that of fulfilling visitor information needs and of visitor management. The ethics and behaviour of tourists are changing, and tourists are now demanding for more environmentally responsible services and products as well as information. Tourists want to learn about the environments they visit as well as understand their associations with a broader environment. Hence, education and interpretation carry out a central role in ecotourism. Through education and interpretation, ecotourists can gain a better understanding, awareness and appreciation of the natural and cultural environment.

It is important to evaluate interpretation programmes to ascertain whether management goals are being met. This chapter identified the market segment of the Selirong Island, visitors" satisfaction levels with the interpretations at the island and how their experience stimulates them to think and develop connections with the island. While display boards are the most desired educative tool for visitors to learn about the environment, leaflets and guides at Selirong Island received a poor impression by visitors. Although the interpretive experience made the visitors think about the issues presented, they would not necessarily talk about the issues to others. The findings, hence, suggested that most of the visitors did not necessarily have a high quality experience with the existing interpretation and that conservation messages are not effectively conveyed by park managers at the island. Selirong Island has the potential to become an ecotourism and a recreational tourism destination, and a platform where conservation and environmental education can be imparted, but this will require a massive effort from the park managers to make it happen.

REFERENCES

Agbayani, C.V., De Silva, M.W.R.N., & Sahat, H.M.J. (1992). Island management strategy for Brunei Darussalam. In: Silvestre, G., Jaafar, H.M., Yussof, P.S.P.H., De Silva, M.W.R.N., & Chua, T.E. (Eds.). *The coastal resources of Brunei Darussalam: Status, utilization and management* (pp. 143-154). Brunei Darussalam: Ministry of Development and Philippines: ICLARM.

Ahmad, A. (2002). Tourism. In: Ibrahim, S.H., Abu Salim, K., Charles, J.K., Ahmad, A., & Lane, D.J.W. (Eds.). *Proposed management plan for Pulau Selirong*. Brunei Darussalam: Ministry of Industry and Primary Resources and Japan: Ramsar Centre.

Ahmad, A. (2008). Understanding the impacts of ecotourism in Brunei Darussalam: Views of the visitors. In: Pillarisetti, J.R., Lawrey, R., Teo, S.Y., Siddiqui, S. & Ahmad, A. (Eds.). *Small economies and global economics* (pp. 189-202). New York: Nova Science.

Ahmad, A. (2015). Conservation of island biodiversity in Brunei Darussalam: The role of ecotourism in environmental education. *International Journal of Ecology and Development, 30*(1), 51-63.

Anderson, J.A.R., & Marsden, J.D. (1984). *Forest resources and strategic planning study.* Brunei Darussalam: Government of Brunei Darussalam.

Ceballos-Lascuráin, H. (1991). Tourism, ecotourism and protected areas. *Parks, 2*(3), 31-35.

Ceballos-Lascuráin, H. (1996). *Tourism, ecotourism and protected areas: The state of nature-based tourism around the world and guidelines for its development.* Gland: IUCN and UK: Cambridge.

Charles, J.K. (2002). Pulau Selirong: A forest reserve and an ecotourist destination. In: Kashio, M., Wong, T.M., & Nakamura, R. (Eds.). *Treasures unknown: Proceedings of the experts consultative meeting on managing Pulau Selirong Forest Recreational Park,* 8-10 April 2002 (pp. 71-74). Brunei Darussalam: Forestry Department.

d'Hauteserre, A-M. (2003). A response to „Misguided policy initiatives in small-island destinations: why do upmarket tourism policies fail?" by Dimitri Ioannides and Briavel Holcomb. *Tourism Geographies, 5*(1), 49-53.

Government of Brunei Darussalam. (1958). *Annual Report.* Brunei Darussalam: Government of Brunei Darussalam.

Government of Brunei Darussalam. (1966). *Annual Report.* Brunei Darussalam: Government of Brunei Darussalam.

Government of Brunei Darussalam. (1967). *Annual Report.* Brunei Darussalam: Government of Brunei Darussalam.

Government of Brunei Darussalam. (2007). *Brunei Darussalam long-term development plan.* Brunei Darussalam: Prime Minister's Office.

Griffin, T. & Archer, D. (2001). *Visitor Study 1999-2000: Northern NSW National Parks.* Prepared for New South Wales National Parks and Wildlife Service, Northern Directorate, Grafton by University of Technology, Sydney.

Ham, S. H. (2007). Can interpretation really make a difference? Answers to four questions from cognitive and behavioral psychology. *Interpreting world heritage conference.* Vancouver, Canada. 25-29 March 2007.

Hughes, M. & Morrison-Saunders, A. (2005). Influence of on-site interpretation intensity on visitors to natural areas. *Journal of Ecotourism, 4*(3), 161–177.

Ibrahim, S.H. (2002). A socio-economic study of Selirong Island, Brunei Darussalam. In: Kashio, M., Wong, T.M., & Nakamura, R. (Eds.).

Treasures unknown: Proceedings of the experts consultative meeting on managing Pulau Selirong Forest Recreational Park, 8-10 April 2002 (pp. 66-70). Brunei Darussalam: Forestry Department.

Ibrahim, S.H., & Ahmad, A. (2002). *Welcome to Pulau Selirong: A visitor's guide*. Brunei Darussalam: Forestry Department and RCJ.

Jacobs, M. H. & Harms, M. (2014). Influence of interpretation on conservation intentions of whale tourists. *Tourism Management, 42*, 123–131.

Kaltenborn, B. P., Nyahongo, J. W. & Kideghesho, J. R. (2011). The attitudes of tourists towards the environmental, social and managerial attributes of Serengeti National Park, Tanzania. *Tropical Conservation Science, 4*(2), 132–148.

Kashio, M. (2002). Scope of work: what to do and where to go? In: Kashio, M., Wong, T.M., & Nakamura, R. (Eds.). *Treasures unknown: Proceedings of the experts' consultative meeting on managing Pulau Selirong Forest Recreational Park*, 8-10 April 2002 (pp. 14-17). Brunei Darussalam: Forestry Department.

Lindberg, K., & Hawkins, D.E. (1993). *Ecotourism: A guide for planners and managers*. North Bennington, Vermont: The Ecotourism Society.

Madin, E.M.P., & Fenton, D.M. (2004). Environmental interpretation in the Great Barrier Marine Reef Park: An assessment of programme effectiveness. *Journal of Sustainable Tourism, 12*(2), 121-137.

Masli, U. (2010, July 4). First mangrove centre likely on Selirong Island. *The Brunei Times*. Retrieved from http://www.bt.com.bn/news-national/2010/07/04/first-mangrove-centre-likely-selirong-island

Munro, J. K., Morrison-Saunders, A. & Hughes, M. (2008). Environmental interpretation evaluation in natural areas. *Journal of Ecotourism, 7*(1), 1–14.

Orams, M.B. (1996). Using interpretation to manage nature-based tourism. *Journal of Sustainable Tourism, 4*(2), 81-94.

Reingold, L. (1993). Identifying the elusive ecotourist in *Going Green, a supplement to Tour and Travel News*, 25 October: pp. 36-39.

Thien, R. (2010, January 9). Brunei still has 78% green cover. *The Brunei Times*. Retrieved from http://www.bt.com.bn/news-national/2010/01/09/brunei-still-has-78-green-cover

Too, D. (2014, May 1). MIPR promotes Brunei as ecotourism destination. *The Brunei Times*. Retrieved from http://www.bt.com.bn/business-national/2014/05/01/mipr-promotes-brunei-ecotourism-destination

Tourism Development Department. (2014). *Tourist arrival 2004-2013*. Brunei Darussalam: Ministry of Industry and Primary Resources.

Walker, K. & Moscardo, G. (2014). Encouraging sustainability beyond the tourist experience: ecotourism, interpretation and values. *Journal of Sustainable Tourism, 22*(8), 1175–1196.

Wearing, S., Edinborough, P., Hodgson, L. & Frew, E. (2008). *Enhancing visitor experience through interpretation: An examination of influencing factors.* Gold Coast, Queensland: CRC for Sustainable Tourism.

Weaver, D.B. (2005). Comprehensive and minimalist dimensions of ecotourism. *Annals of Tourism Research, 32*(2), 439-455.

Weiler, B., & Davis, D. (1993). An exploratory investigation into the roles of the nature-based tour leader. *Tourism Management, 14*(2), 91-98.

World Tourism Organisation (WTO). (1998). *Guide for local authorities on developing sustainable tourism.* Madrid: WTO.

World Travel and Tourism Council. (2014). *Travel and tourism economic impact 2014: Brunei Darussalam.* London: WTTC.

Zamora, P. (1987). Mangroves. In: Chua, T.E., Chou, L.M., & Sadorra, M.S.M. (Eds.). *The coastal environmental profile of Brunei Darussalam: Resource assessment and management issues* (pp. 28-43). Brunei Darussalam: Ministry of Development and Philippines: ICLARM.

In: Ecotourism
Editor: Shannon C. Brophy

ISBN: 978-1-63482-027-1
© 2015 Nova Science Publishers, Inc.

Chapter 3

MANAGEMENT OF THE VISITATION IMPACTS AT THE NATIONAL PARK OF CAMPOS GERAIS/BRAZIL: THE CASE OF MARIQUINHA'S WATERFALL

Lilian Vieira Miranda Garcia[1],
Jasmine Cardozo Moreira[1]
and Robert C. Burns[,2]*
[1]Universidade Estadual de Ponta Grossa, Brazil
[2]West Virginia University, Morgantown, WV, US

The Campos Gerais National Park, situated in southern Brazil, was created in 2006 with the aim of conserving the last remaining ecosystems of native grasslands and Araucaria Forest; the phytogeographical area of Atlantic Forest biome. Campos Gerais National Park (CGNP) is one of 68 Brazilian national parks. It is managed by the Chico Mendes Institute for Biodiversity Conservation (ICMBio) as an IUCN (International Union for Conservation of Nature) Category II conservation unit. Although resource protection is a critical management focus at CGNP, public use activities are also very popular within the conservation area. Public use has the potential to generate significant negative impacts to the natural environment and the quality of the visitor's experience if not managed appropriately. Accordingly, this case study

---
* Correspondence: (Office) 304-293-6781; (fax) 304-293-2441

is an analysis of visitation activities and their impacts at Mariquinha Waterfall, one of the most important and most-visited attractions in Campos Gerais National Park (CGNP). Resource managers used the Visitor Impact Management (VIM) process in planning this study which focuses intensely on visitor experiences and the protection of natural and cultural resources. VIM is a visitor monitoring framework used as a guideline for collecting and organizing data, assisting with the management actions related to visitor impact, and serves to support the decisions made by managers. The results of this study showed distinct differences in seasonal visitation at places such as the Mariquinha Waterfall, while other tourist resources in the area receive lower use. Furthermore, managers identified a younger local audience that seeks contact with nature. Most importantly, the study considered both existing and potential tourism activities in the area, with the idea of providing the user a range of possible activities. In conclusion, our findings recommend that efforts should be invested to further study and develop tourism opportunities in natural areas in this park.

1. PROTECTION OF BIODIVERSITY AND VISITATION IN PROTECTED AREAS IN BRAZIL

The Atlantic Forest biome is a set of forest types and associated ecosystems that spans from the southeastern Brazilian coast to the interior of the country. Originally, this biome covered 17 of the 26 Brazilian states. However, just eight percent of the original area exists today (Brazilian Institute of Environment and Renewable Natural Resources, 2010).

Historically, Brazil's conservation units were initiated to protect Brazil's beautiful but fragile natural resources. Brazil's first national park, Itatiaia National Park, was created in 1937 for the purpose of protecting the biome that was under considerable threat. This was followed by the creation of national parks in Iguaçu and the Orgãos Mountain Range in 1939 (Milano, 1985). This first set of conservation units was followed by over 350 additional protected areas across Brazil that make up the current ICMBio system. The system was created in accordance with the requirements set forth by the IUCN, which aims at improving livelihoods of resident native populations within parks. Accordingly, protecting the livelihoods and culture of traditional communities and ensuring sustainable use of resources becomes a state concern (Brasil, 2004).

Similar to the US Organic Act, that effectively authorized the creation of US National Parks (US Government, 1916), the Law of the National System of Conservation Units (SNUC), established in 2000, allowed for the organization of Brazilian Conservation Units. These Conservation Units (CUs) are categorized into 12 categories focusing on conservation as well as the preservation and protection of traditional ways of life. Each CU has specific goals and levels of specified use. The Brazilian CU system is considered one of the most sophisticated models of conservation in the world, as its conception goes beyond maintaining biodiversity by allowing multiple uses of land and natural resources (MMA, 2011).

ICMBio is the federal agency responsible for the management of all federal CUs. These CUs include 71 national parks and an additional 320 units located in all Brazilian biomes and cover approximately 76 million hectares. Twenty-three of these parks are located in the Atlantic Forest, including Campos Gerais National Park- home of the Mariquinha Waterfall. The SNUC law mandates that CUs aim to preserve natural ecosystems of great ecological significance and scenic beauty, to conduct scientific research, to develop environmental education and interpretation activities and to focus on ensuring that Brazilians have the opportunity to experience outdoor recreation and nature-based tourism. (Brasil, 2004).

Public use in Brazil's natural settings is not exclusive to its national parks. Visitation occurs in Brazil's national forests and extractive reserves, both of which are multiple use settings that include timber management, mineral extraction, and others. Similar to many other nations, the national parks are the gems of Brazilian natural resource areas, and much of the nation's natural area visitation occurs within the national parks.

Accordingly, it is imperative that management of Brazil's national parks promote the preservation through activities that strengthen the bond between people and the natural environment. By focusing on the link between visitors and the environment, we can build a sense of stewardship, which is an important step in managing and protecting ICMBio conservation units.

Currently, tourism is one of the largest industries in the world and shows consistent and steady growth. The segment of ecotourism focuses on sustainability, cultural heritage, encouraging conservation, promoting environmental awareness through interpretation, and advocating the welfare of the people involved. According to the World Tourism Organization (UNWTO), ecotourism is growing three times faster than any other sector of tourism (EMBRATUR, 1994; Forest Foundation, 2010a). Since some of the most beautiful landscapes in Brazil are protected management areas, visitation is at a high demand (Nelson, 2012). As further evidence of this growing demand, ICMBio data indicates that visitation in National Parks increased about 330% between the years 2006 and 2013 (ICMBio, 2014). Furthermore, visitation targets were exceeded during the past two years. The increase in visitors and growth of the ecotourism industry in Brazil further reinforce the need for a Public Use Plan to organize visitation within Conservation Units. This Public Use Plan should focus on improving visitation quality and minimizing the impacts generated by recreation activities. Additionally, it is necessary to build clear goals for public use of UCs and to conduct studies analyzing the impacts of visitation that will assist managers of these protected areas.

2. MANAGEMENT OF IMPACTS VISITATION AT UC IN BRAZIL

The management of visitation activities is extremely important in reaching conservation goals. Measurements of activity restriction and the influence on visitation behaviors should be taken to minimize negative impacts and improve experiential quality. Institutional tools for measuring and managing the impacts of public use areas were first applied in the United States and were adapted by the rest of the world. In Brazil, the institutional tools for planning and managing the impacts of visitation have been a recent development. The Forest Foundation, which manages the CUs in the State of São Paulo, published a tool based on the VIM (Visitor Impact Management) method in 2010- the Monitoring Plan of Visitor Management Impacts (Forest Foundation, 2010b).

In 2011, ICMBio released the Methodology for Management of Impacts of Visitation that focused on visitors" experiences and the protection of natural and cultural resources. Reference tools for this plan included the Recreation Opportunity Spectrum (ROS), Carrying Capacity, Limits of Acceptable Change (LAC), Visitor Experience and Resource Protection (VERP) and Visitor Impact Management (VIM) (ICMBio, 2011). Both instruments were initially applied in the Conservation Units, and often are not used in research. Looking at the history of public use management tool implementation, one can see that the improvement of these instruments is a continuous process that is dependent on application, verification and review. If parks and protected areas are not used to their potential, they can become irrelevant to society. If parks are over-used or poorly managed, there will be other negative results. For these reasons, making use of existing visitor impact management tools is a critical to the management process. Using the best science available (visitor management frameworks) is the responsibility of both park administrators and public land use researchers (McCool & Lime, 2001).

The following figure (Figure 1) depicts the development of management tools as well as their origins and guiding principles.

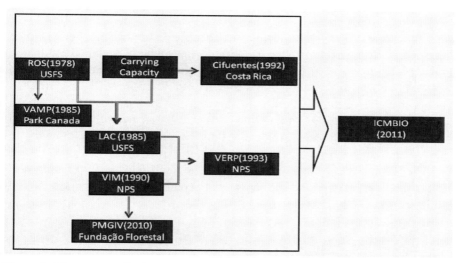

Figure 1. Management Tools.

The key factor of the ICMBio method is defining and monitoring the impacts of visitation indicators on the quality of the environment and the experience of visitors. Management is understood as a cyclical and self-fed process, meaning that the results of the process are raw materials for the improvement of the next cycle. So this tool is divided into the following five stages: organization and planning, diagnosis and prioritization of activities, establishment of NBV (Bollard number of the Visitation), monitoring and evaluation indicators and management actions. This process includes impact monitoring, identification of spatial features/structures, activities and their impacts beyond a typical visitor profile survey. The analysis of this data supports the monitoring plan by focusing on the best methods of conducting a thorough, quality survey. In fact, all activities that cause impacts to the natural environment or to visitation quality should receive management actions. However, the operational capacity of parks does not always permit this level of management. Therefore, the priority matrix of management actions is essential in determining the most critical problems that require attention.

The study at Mariquinha Waterfall, in Campos Gerais National Park, is an example of using this methodology for diagnosing and prioritizing management actions as well as implementing a monitoring plan.

3. CAMPOS GERAIS NATIONAL PARK

In the state of Paraná, located in southern Brazil, the Atlantic Forest biome has several In the state of Paraná, located in southern Brazil, the Atlantic Forest biome has several vegetation types (Figure 2). The area on which two vegetation types, the Natural Field and Mixed Rainforest (FOM), meet is known that the Araucaria Forest. In Paraná, this area is known as Campos Gerais. Guimarães (2009, p.48) defined this area as "an area originally covered by grasslands and forests, Araucaria Pine Forest grows predominantly in shallow and sandy soils."

The "uniqueness of this biogeographical region (fields, forests, soil types, etc.) is directly linked to the geological and geomorphological characteristics" (Guimarães et al., 2007 p.32).

Figure 2: São Jorge Waterfall – View of Campos Gerais, Paraná.

Data indicates that this type of forest vegetation is among the most endangered vegetation types in the Atlantic Forest with no more than 1% of its original area remaining today. The loss of natural vegetation of Araucaria Forest is due to a history of intense logging, conversion of areas for livestock, agriculture and reforestation with exotic species. The latter is currently a major threat to the returning native species. All of these reasons served as the catalyst for the creation of protected areas in the region. (Medeiros, Savi & Brito, 2005).

As a result, Campos Gerais National Park was created in 2006. This CU aims at preserving the remnants of the Araucaria Forest and native grassland, in addition to facilitating research and the development of eco-tourism and environmental education. (Brasil, 2006).

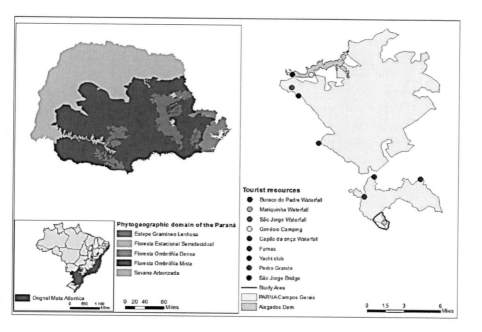

Figure 3: Area Map - Vegetation and tourist attractions.

The natural attractions within Campos Gerais National Park have been seen as natural resource features for generations of Brazilians. Before the designation of the Park, tourism was already present within the region. Some of the attractions are still managed by the owners or tenants, depending on whether the CU land regularization process was completed. Currently, visitation has no emphasis on environmental sustainability and individual activities themselves. In order to comply with ICMBio's objectives, namely preserving biodiversity and improving visitation quality, the consolidated tourist areas of the CU must meet standards for minimizing impacts. The area of this study, Mariquinha Waterfall, is one of six tourist areas within Campos Gerais that fails to meet these standards (Figure 3).

The need for evaluation is justified not only on the basis of minimizing the impacts of tourism, but also because of the different activity objectives within the National Park and in areas that are not governed by the SNUC system (National System Conservation Units).

3.1. Mariquinha Waterfall: Diagnosis for Adequacy of Public Use

The area around Mariquinha Waterfall, located about 30 km from the rural city of Ponta Grossa, includes a network of short trails, both marked and unmarked, that give tourists access to the waterfall and other resources.

Between January and October 2014, the site received about 2,825 visitors (Figure 4). The data shows a very strong trend in seasonal visitation. This presents a problem for the economic viability of the area in that facilities must be designed to accommodate high use, but must also be maintained during periods of low use.

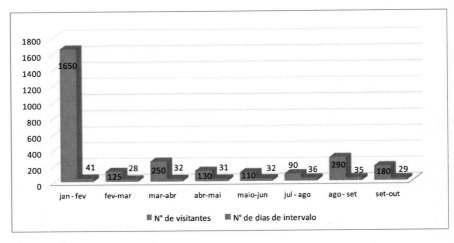

Figure 4. Annual Visitation at Mariquinha Waterfall.

Examining both the spatial layout of the area and information related to activities allows for a better understanding of the area's use dynamics. The map below (Figure 5) shows the spatial features of the area.

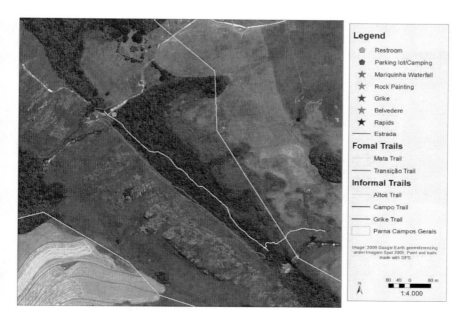

Figure 5. Study Area Map.

3.1.1. Tourism Resources

As previously mentioned, the most popular feature in the study area is the Mariquinha Waterfall (Figure 6). The waterfall is the site where the Quebra-Perna River falls 30 meters to the rocky, shallow river bed below. However other, lesser used sites, have been included in this study for their tourism potential. One example of such a site is the Rift (Figure 7), an area of rock formations, fissures and a waterfall with beach access. Additionally, there is a complex of smaller waterfalls above the Mariquinha Waterfall. Both of these areas may not be known to the general public because of the lack of signage and trail markers. Their locations within the area make them great potential attractions and help to reduce the amount of visitation related impacts at the main waterfall.

Another potential tourism resource is ancient sandstone inscriptions (rock paintings) that have been found in various locations within the study area.

However, visitors that have accessed this inscriptions have vandalized or stolen them, thus taking away the cultural heritage in some areas (Figure 6). This behavior could be remedied through interpretive projects that could potentially reduce destructive behaviors and promote use in the area during seasons when cooler temperatures prevent swimming in the waterfalls.

Figure 6. Tourism Resources of Mariquinha Waterfall.

3.1.2. Structures, Activities and Impacts

Among the five areas analyzed in the study, all had some degree of visitor-related impact. The lack of trail markers and creation of social trails has caused widespread damage to vegetation, human injury related to falls, and has increased the risk of contact with venomous animals. However, developing some of these social trails can spread out use on existing trails and provide opportunities to view flora and fauna, peculiar geology, rock paintings and alternate views of the waterfall (Figure 7). Developing these additional trails can also help preserve more of the natural areas.

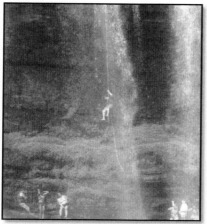

Figure 7: Structures and Activities.

The study area has two locations designated for parking and camping (Figure 7). It is not possible to identify conflicts between day users and overnight users because the camping areas are rarely used. However, the impacts of both activities on the natural environment are evident, especially the use of fires. Unsupervised fires could spread to areas of native grass. Additionally, improper waste disposal causes both a visual impact to the area and threatens the health of wildlife. In other Brazilian National Parks, such as the Iguaçu National Park and Serra dos Orgaos National Park, human food and discarded packaging causes a terribly negative impact on the local fauna.

The most popular activity for visitors at the Mariquinha Waterfall is swimming and wading in the river. The negative impacts of water recreation in the Quebra-Perna River are not evident. However the number of people, especially in the area of the main waterfall, can decrease the quality of visitation. The seasonality of public use in the area is a reflection of the type of activity that visitors seek. As a result, it is important to plan and provide new facilities that encourage increased visitation during months with lower temperatures.

Another activity with the potential to grow in popularity is cascading; a unique activity in which recreationists rappel down the vertical cliff within a waterfall. Although some conflict between the cascaders and swimmers was reported. One set back is that cascading is regarded as an adventure tourism activity and further development of facilities for this activity will require certified instructors and insurance (The Brazilian Adventure Tourism Association, Ministry of Tourism, 2009).

3.1.3. Visitor Profile

The visitor profile survey gave researchers a detailed understanding of the people that come to the waterfalls as well as their expectations and experiences. Such data is essential for planning improvements and the development of new facilities that enhance visitation quality.

Generally, most of the visitors to natural areas are youth and young adults. The visitors at the Mariquinha Waterfall are no different with 81.6% of respondents being between the ages of 18 and 38 (Figure 8). The large presence of visitors in this age group may support the development of interpretive products and adventure tourism activities.

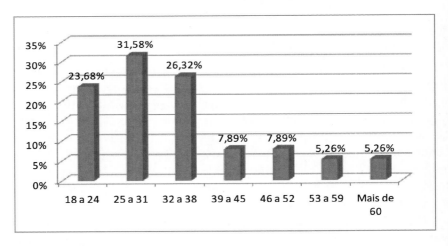

Figure 8. Visitor's age.

The visitors were almost exclusively (94.0%) from cities within the state of Paraná. Most (88.0%) of these visitors indicated that they were from the city of Ponta Grossa. This suggests that residents from Ponta Grossa have a strong place attachment to the study area. The possibility of conserving the natural resource through education and interpretation is high as a result of this place attachment.

Analyzing group size is important both to assess the impact of visitation in natural areas and for the planning, implementation and evaluation of management strategies to facilitate these groups (Barros, 2003). The vast majority (88.36%) of respondents at the Mariquinha Waterfall were in groups of up to ten people (Table 1). This data reflects the trend in group sizes found in other Brazilian parks (Kataoka, 2004; Barros, 2003). Many of the groups at the Mariquinha Waterfall were recreating with families, so it is important to prioritize the planning and implementation of facilities that promote family recreation.

Table 1. Size of groups visiting the waterfall Mariquinha

Group size (%)	
1 a 5	60.5
6 a 10	27.9
Over 10	11.6

The main motivation for visiting the area was to have contact with nature. However, there is a difference in the motivations between first time and repeat visitors. First time visitors were more likely to state that their motivation was to have contact with nature. On the other hand, a larger proportion of repeat visitors came to the area because the liked the waterfall itself (Table 2).

Table 2. Visit's motivation

Visit''s Motivation	First Visit (%)	Second Visit or more (%)
Contact with nature	80.6	40.9
I like Mariquinha Waterfall	-	40.9
Practicing physical activities	3.2	6.8
Spending more time with friends	12.9	9.1
It''s close to my house	-	2.3

3.2. Prioritization of Activities for Management Actions

Based on the ICMBio methodology used in this study, the activities used in this analysis were prioritized for management by visitor demand, obvious potential impacts and management zones. Thus, the visitor demand is calculated from the percentage of users who performed the activity, with more than 70% of users have scores 3, between 40% and 70% have scores 2 and less than 40% has a score of 1 (ICMBio, 2011). Table 3 shows the activities that occur at the Mariquinha Waterfall.

Table 3. Visitor's activities

Activities in which I Participated (%)	
Trekking	100
Parking	100
Mariquinha Waterfall swimming	74.4
Barbecue	16.3
Picnic	12.8
Camping	4.6
Waterfall Activities	2.3

ICMBio evaluates impacts by ranking them on a scale of 1-3 (ICMBio, 2011). A score of one means that there is no discernible impact. A score of two means little apparent impact. Finally, a score of three means visible impacts are present. To obtain a final impact score, the ranking is multiplied by two. Management zones are assigned to sites within the study area. However, the Campos Gerais National Park has no management plan and, therefore, no zoning. As a result, the entire study area was considered as an area of intensive impact for this study.

As seen in Table 4, indicators of environmental quality and visitation experience were established for each of the activities. By examining these indicators and considering the acceptable conditions, strategies can be formulated to minimize impacts.

Table 4. Impact priorization of management actions

Activities	Visitor"s demand	Clear Impacts (X2)	Management Zone	Total
Trekking	3	6	1	16
Mariquinha Waterfall Bath	3	6	1	16
Barbecue	1	6	1	14
Parking	3	4	1	12
Picnic	1	4	1	10
Camping	1	2	1	6
Waterfall Activities	1	2	1	6

CONCLUSION

The concern of protecting the Atlantic Forest biome was a recurring theme before the creation of the first Brazilian conservation unit. With the growth of ecotourism in Brazil comes a sustainable alternative to safely use the last remnants of this biome.

Some of the most beautiful Brazilian landscapes are in protected areas, especially in the National Parks. These parks seek to protect the natural area through developing ecotourism opportunities, interpretation and environmental education programs.

As a result, the examination of visitation activities is extremely important for the planning and development of public use. This use should correlate with the guidelines and objectives of ICMBio protected areas and for the sustainability of the activities themselves.

Public use within the National Parks should be viewed as an opportunity to bring society to the natural environment, support and preserve the heritage of the area as well as strengthen the overall National System of Protected Areas. Various tools should be utilized in minimizing the negative impacts and promoting positive impacts. Thus paving the way to reach the goal of why the protected area was established in the first place.

REFERENCES

Barros, M. (2003). Characterization of visitation, visitors and assessment of the ecological and recreational impacts of upland Itatiaia National Park

(Master of Forest Resources Dissertation). University of São Paulo, Piracicaba.

Brazil Adventure Tourism Association: Tourism Ministry (2009). Good practice handbook: Safe adventure, canyoneering and waterfall-rappelling. Belo Horizonte: Ministry of Tourism, 53.

Brazil Federal Decree n 23 (March 2006). Creation of the Campos Gerais National Park. Brasilia: Senate, 10.

Brazil Law No. 9985 of July 18, 2000. National Protected Areas System - Law of the National System of Conservation Units. Brasilia: Environmental State Secretary. (2004), 56.

Brazilian Institute of Environment and Renewable Natural Resources. (2010). Atlantic Forest: National heritage of Brazilians. Brasilia: Federal Environmental Ministry 2010, 408.

Brazilian Tourism Institute /Brazilian Institute of Environment and Renewable Natural Resources. (1994). Guidelines for a national ecotourism policy. Brasilia: Brazilian Tourism Institute.

Federal Environmental Ministry. Ten years of the national system of protected areas of nature lessons of the past, present achievements and future prospects. Brasilia: Federal Environmental Ministry (2011), 171.

Forest Foundation (2010a). Ecotourism: Environmental Education Pad, São Paulo: City Hall, 43.

Forest Foundation (2010b) (Manual monitoring and management of visitation impacts in protected areas. São Paulo: Environmental State Secretary, 78.

Guimaraes, G. B., Melo, M. S., Giannini, P. C. F., & Melek, P. R. (2007). Campos Gerais Geology. In: Melo, M. S., Moro, R. (Eds). *Natural Heritage General Paraná Fields*. Ponta Grossa: UEPG, 23-32.

Guimaraes, G.B. (2009). Challenges of geoconservation in General Paraná fields. *Journal of the Institute of Geosciences of USP, São Paulo*. 5, 47-61.

ICMBio (Chico Mendez Institute). Management report: 2013. Brasilia: ICMBio (2014), 238. Available at: Retrieved 09/10/2014 from http://www.icmbio.gov.br/portal/quem-somos/relatorios-de-gestao.

_____. Methodological roadmap for visitation impacts management: Focusing on visitor experience and protection of natural and cultural resources. Brasilia: ICMBio (2011), 88.

Kataoka, S.Y. (2004). Indicators of quality visitor experience at the State Park of Anchieta Island, RJ. (Master of Forest Resources Dissertation) University of São Paulo. Piracicaba.

McCool, S.F. & Lime, D.W. (2001) Tourism carrying capacity: Tempting fantasy or useful reality? *Journal of Sustainable Tourism*, *9*(5), 372-388.

Medeiros, J. D., Savi, M., & Brito, B. F. A. (2005). Selection of areas for the creation of protected areas in the mixed rain forest. *Biotemas Florianópolis*, *18*(2), 33-50.

Milano, M.S. (1985). Parks and reserves: an analysis of Brazilian politics of conservation units. *Curitiba Forest Magazine*, 15(*12*), 4-9.

Nelson, S. (2012). Public use in protected areas. *In* WWF Brazil, IPE. Protected Areas Management: Sharing a training experience. 1st Ed Brasilia: WWF (2012), 215-237.

The National Park Service Organic Act. (1916), *The National Park Service Organic Act 16*, U.S.C. 1 2 3, and 4.

In: Ecotourism
Editor: Shannon C. Brophy

ISBN: 978-1-63482-027-1
© 2015 Nova Science Publishers, Inc.

Chapter 4

ECOTOURISM IN COLOMBIA

Fernando Ramírez[1], *
and Julio Cesar Augusto Pinzón[2]
[1]Facultad de Ciencias Sociales, Universidad Colegio Mayor
de Cundinamarca, Bogotá, Colombia
[2]Departamento de Filosofía, Universidad Pedagógica Nacional,
Bogotá, Colombia

ABSTRACT

Colombia is considered one of the most biodiversity and cultural rich countries worldwide. The origin of ecotourism as a field in Colombia can be traced back to the early 1908s. Ecotourism has been hampered by corruption and pseudo-ecotourism based industries that focus on making large economic revenues that are not environmentally sound. Ecotourism research has been carried on a regional and local level in the Amazonas, Cundinamarca and Boyacá States among other regions. Currently, few research organizations are involved in ecotourism and few offer reliable plans for ecotourists. Recently, research in wetland ecotourism has provided elements to construct a reliable wetland restoration and conservation framework. This ecotourism framework provides the first opportunity to consistently manage wetland sites and propose real solutions to these highly threatened ecosystems. This chapter focuses on the recent and past advances on the field of ecotourism in Colombia. It

* Corresponding author: framirezl@unicolmayor.edu.co (F. Ramírez).

explores ecotourism related aspects in the context of philosophy, biodiversity, culture, research, policy, education, ethics, conflict related aspects.

Keywords: Environment, birds, South America, ecotourists, biodiversity, culture

INTRODUCTION

Colombia is unique country because it harbors a rich biodiversity and cultural background. Colombia is catalogued as a megadiverse country (Saenz et al., 2013). This biodiversity is represented partly by endemic species which are unique to the country and are not found elsewhere in the world. Colombia has numerous unique ecosystems that stretch from the northern coastal regions bordering the Caribbean Ocean such as the Sierra Nevada de Santa Marta, which is the world's highest coastal mountain rage, originating at sea level and rising to 5,775 meters above sea level, to the dazzling rainforests in the Choco region that borders the Pacific Ocean. The Choco phytogeographical region of coastal Colombia and adjacent Ecuador is well known as a region of unusually high endemism in plants, birds, and butterflies (Gentry, 1986) and among them, perhaps one of the wettest places of the world namely, Tutunendo, perhaps the rainiest place in the world, 11,770 mm (Gentry, 1986).

Stretching on the southern part of the country the Amazon rain forest is one of Colombia's majestic regions. Harboring unique ecosystems such as the Igapos or Blackwater stream systems that are home to numerous species. For example, a great diversity of fishes has been observed among these streams, some of them with unique dietary- morphological specializations (Ramírez and Davenport 2015 in press). Stretching over the Eastern Cordillera, the vast savanna called the llanos is found, which harbors a great biodiversity. Here, it is possible to observe the unique spectacle of freshwater dolphins found in the Mancacias, Yucao and Meta Rivers. The Llanos region stretches over to neighboring Venezuela, where the "llanero" local people and indigenous cultures live in harmony with this marvelous environment. The massif mountain system known as the Andes initiates on the southern part of the country at the Nudo de Los Pastos region that divides into the three cordilleras. The Andes is home to the endangered Spectacle bear, and one of Colombia's distinguished icons, the Andes condor, an endangered species that thrives over the high altitude mountain ranges. Colombia offers much more relevant places, biodiversity and unique cultures that make it an overwhelmingly interesting location for the tourism and ecotourism sector.

Aside from the rich biodiversity, Colombia is characterized by a rich cultural diversity. Moreover, is home to 80 indigenous cultures (Hudson, 2010). Most of these cultures are remnants of large groups that were reduced due to the Spaniard colonization and the mixing process. Today the indigenous groups play an important role as guardians and protectors of nature. The ample amiability and generosity of the current local groups makes Colombia an interesting destination for travelers worldwide. Although, violence and social instability occur in some regions (as consequence of illegal armed groups as guerilla and paramilitary illicit forces), other parts of the country offer possibilities for visitors.

The development of ecotourism in Colombia dates back to the 1980s. During that time, political decisions created the first National Park System. Since that time, the ecotourism sector has become a growing economic sector, but sadly it has been influenced by *mercantilism* ideas that seek only economic revenues leaving aside the core philosophy of ecotourism. The philosophy of ecotourism is a key point that needs to be defined in Colombia. The philosophy of ecotourism needs to fulfil the many gaps that occur between the tour providers, the private and public sectors as well as the tourists and ecotourists. Another important aspect is education, which stands as one of the elements that must be met in an efficient ecotourism program to push forward.

This chapter explores recent and past advances in the field of ecotourism in Colombia. It explores ecotourism related aspects in the context of philosophy, biodiversity, culture, research, policy, education, ethics, conflict related aspects.

PHILOSOPHY: ELEMENTS TO REFLECT IN ECOTOURISM

Thinking about ecological issues in today's world requires a great amount of serenity. This is based on two reasons, first, because it is difficult to achieve consciousness about the planet's great destruction, and second, because of the great generalized indifference around what this means in the life of all beings that inhabit the world.

Over time, we have lived accustomed to produce garbage. Moreover, over all the places we visit, we leave this negative mark. This causes pollution which in turn, causes destruction and fouls the site that was originally beautiful, nice, clean and healthy. Moreover, after a swimmer group of people visits the beach, the place is left disastrous. This is the sad reality occurring in Colombia (Figure 1).

Figure 1. Coveñas, Colombia. Photo by Julio Cesar Augusto Pinzón.

The tourism industry and the way tourists think is often influenced by the idea of obtaining large economic revenues and benefits. This view often forgets that nature needs great care in the way we behave with it. Most people traveling in search of rest never stop and think about nature''s care. Most people seem distracted over the trip''s itinerary, the hotel''s comfort, the tourist''s attractions, and end up ignoring the environmental reality of the visited place. No one warns, informs, orients about the ecological neglected issues. We lack education, and even, national and state authorities in Colombia have a careless attitude towards tourism based destinations. These destinations are singular because they are not found elsewhere in the world. Colombia has a number of unique aspects. For example, climates, landscapes, biodiversity, etc. Moreover, Colombia has plant and animal species that are not found in other parts of the world and people that do not know and care little about these natural resources. Developing new human attitudes towards the ecological reality in Colombia requires time, monetary investment and people with a high solidarity ideology. People in Colombia need an ecotourism-based consciousness. This is to know clearly what is meant by ecotourism. The root of the word ecotourism refers to ecology and to the tourist''s attractions or the traveler''s interest. There are many ecotourism definitions, but most do not focus on the ideological approach problems inherent to the word ecotourism.

For example, the ideal of beauty we take it from Aristotle (Aristóteles, 1999) and apply it to ecotourism.

It all begins when we understand that life manifests in life. This is, the life in our planet is unfathomable, unlimited, and permanent. The real essence of all that exists, at least for us humans is directed by a superior being understood as a supreme being that is a distinct reality from that of the world and from the world's things. It is not possible to escape from the reality called life, it is impossible to live without a habitat, we know what we consider real based on life itself (Plotino, 1985). If we comprehend that life is one, unique, and that we are not life's creators. Moreover, being the owners of a superior intelligence in nature we are called to take care of it and conserve it.

What is meant to live according to nature? According to Cleanthes, a Stoic philosopher, to live according to nature, is to define what good consists of and the purpose of human life (Cavallé, 2006). According to Cavallé (2006), the nature of human thinking is understood as the principle that sustains the world and as the unique law of all natural laws. Nature, therefore, is to know how to live in conformity, harmony and wisdom as we are identified with nature, nature is not a blind reality, but a source of light where human intelligence arises, and because human intelligence is the fabric of things we do not need to make sense of things that already make sense, the unique sense. When we make sense of things, e.g., sacred respect for the Earth, for our body, for the planet, animals and all Biorhythms, nature shows us that they are wise within their reality. This reflection invites us not to forget that *Life, Love* and *Intelligence* are the intimate reality of all things and thus, we cannot remain as simple spectators of its laws and rhythms, but we need to adapt to them in a humble way. Here is, where the contrast is astonishing, we can all see the consequences of human intervention in the natural world, wherein the name of science or a technique, intimacy is not respected nor considered, the laws the rhythms are not taken seriously, and then we ask ourselves cynically for the cause of the soil's sterility, the land, water and air pollution, without forgetting the fauna and flora annihilation. Philosophers say almost nothing. Philosophers should know and know how the respect begins by respecting plants, animals, water and land. Philosophers wanting to be the alarm voice are not heard. Wisdom teaches that human beings are not isolated beings from the whole of life, but the place where the cosmos can become fully aware, that is why we are responsible for caring for the environment and nature. This is ecology. This should be our attitude toward the natural world (Cavallé, 2006).

The philosophy of ecotourism in Colombia should be based on the idea that Colombia is a paradise and thus, the people that inhabit the country as well as visitors should visit a tourism place with the consciousness that the place should be conserved intact as originally found. Moreover, we should have knowledge about the place visited, so that we contribute to its natural development of flora and fauna by previous research, which allows us to return the natural beings that have been taken out after years of ecological destruction. This would be the way *to pay* the high price of visiting these nature sacred temples.

Numerous philosophical and political ideologies have contributed to the present form of ecological thought and the formation of the nature travel known today as ecotourism (Wearing and Neil, 1999). Ecotourism philosophy is dominated by western thought, thus many valuable lessons can only be learned by deconstructing its meaning to find application in various socio-cultural contexts (Nowaczek et al., 2007).

The development of an ecotourism philosophy (e.g., For a service provider) requires the examination of some basic assumptions regarding the place of ecotourism in the context of the environment, the nature of human activity, the basis of human nature and the nature of human relationships (Malloy and Fennell 1998a). According to Fennell (2008a) An agency's philosophy, then, is a direct reflection of what the entity values. There are perhaps a series of other core environmental values which would be articulated by ecotourists over other types of tourists, as being fundamental to the travel experience. These may include reducing, reusing and recycling; harmony; exploration; multiculturalism; preservation of landscapes; biodiversity conservation; integrity; learning; service and knowledge (Fennell, 2008a).

BIODIVERSITY ASPECTS

Species richness generally increases with decreasing latitude. Due to this biogeographical phenomenon, the overwhelming majority of species are located in developing countries (WCMC, 1992). Industrialized countries, in contrast, are characterized by high and increasing demand for nature-based vacations, with protected areas representing first-rate attractions. Tourism could therefore be a means of redistributing economic resources, mitigating the socioeconomic situation both at local and national scale and contributing to biodiversity conservation (Budowski, 1976; Gössling, 1999). There is a broad consensus that such tourism should be fully compatible with conservation goals, while at the same time posing the minimum threat to the continuation of local culture and society (Gössling, 1999). Within this context, Colombia, a biodiversity and culturally rich country bordered by two oceans, offers great potential for ecotourism as evidenced by protected areas (Figure 2).

Figure 2. Colombia''s protected areas. Image by Fernando Ramírez.

Colombia is one of the world''s megadiverse countries, hosting about 10-14% of the world''s biodiversity (Saenz et al., 2013; SIB, 2014). Within Colombia, the largest source of biological diversity is found in the Andean ecosystem, characterized by a significant variety of endemic species, followed by the Amazon rainforest and the sub-humid ecosystem in the Chóco bio-geographical area (Saenz et al., 2013). Colombian biodiversity is a source of genetic resources, invaluable cures for human diseases, contemplation, research, spiritual inspiration and philosophical esthetic values, etc., as part of human heritage for present and past generations. For example, Colombia has over 3500 species of orchids (Jørgensen et al., 2011) and among them, the National Flower *Cattleya trianae* Lindl & Rchb. Fil, is one of the most spectacular species (Figure 3), but is currently in danger of extinction due to habitat loss as a consequence of agricultural expansion (Calderón-Sáenz (Ed.), 2006). (See SIB, 2014 for more information on Colombia's biodiversity).

Figure 3. Colombian Orchids. A) *Cathleya trianae*, B) *Odontoglossum luteopurpureum*, C) *Anguloa* sp., D) *Cymbidium* sp., E) *Miltoniopsis* sp. and F) *Doritis* sp. Photos by Fernando Ramírez.

The rich biodiversity is one of the key aspects that is essential for the ecotourism sector. Linking biodiversity and ecotourism provides an interesting field for ecotourists to observe Colombia's natural treasures. However, to date, few initiatives have proposed a link between ecotourism and biodiversity in Colombia. Most tourism operator's work under the name *Ecotourism* without actually knowing the field's, roots or philosophical basis. These operators offer *ecotourism destinations* as a pretext for obtaining large economic revenues from unaware tourists. Moreover, Ospina et al. (2013) found that tour operators and travelers" knowledge on available ecotourism destinations and activities is poor. Marketing activities are inefficient and are characterized as low impact activities at the consumer level. Ecotourism destinations in Colombia lack promotion from tour operators and the tourism industry, except for the Tayrona National Park and the Los Nevados National Park (Ospina et al., 2013).

Colombia occupies 401,042 mi 2 (1,038,699 km^2) of the north western end of South America. Its western shore is bordered by the Pacific Ocean, and its northern shore borders the Atlantic (Ramírez and Davenport, 2013). Inland ecosystems vary from the highland frozen volcanic tops to cool climate Paramos to the warm coastline beaches and rocky shores. A plethora of ecosystems can be found including deserts, dry forests in the coastal region, rain forests in the Amazon, vast savannas in the Orinoco and different elevation zones on the Andes mountain system.

Colombia also ranks as one of the world"s richest countries in aquatic resources represented by numerous rivers, streams, floodplains, lakes and lagoons and massive sub-continental river basins such as Amazon, Orinoco, the Magdalena and Cauca (Saenz et al., 2013; Ramírez and Davenport, 2013). The ecotourism sector has a wide range of opportunities, but few have been explored.

Ecotourism by nature, and often by definition, is a form of tourism that takes place primarily in natural areas (Fennell, 2008b). Ecotourism is often viewed as effective for promoting the conservation of endangered species and habitats in developing countries (Bookbinder et al., 1998). Biodiversity has been considered an important attribute used in ecotourism definitions. For example, Ceballos-Lascuráin was among the first to coin the term *Ecotourism* as „traveling to relatively undisturbed or uncontaminated natural areas with the specific objective of studying, admiring, and enjoying the scenery and its wild plants and animals, as well as any existing cultural manifestations (both past and present) found in these areas"(Boo 1990).

This definition implies that visitors are interested in biodiversity as aspects manifested as plant and animals. Moreover, the foundation of ecotourism may be directly linked to conservation and environmentalism, but there is a cultural component to Cebellos-Lascuráin"s definition suggesting that it is not only about natural history and protected areas, but also about the people who live and have lived in these places (Fennell, 2008b).

Ecotourism most likely has a convergent evolution, where many places and people independently responded to the need for more nature, travel opportunities in line with society"s efforts to become more ecologically minded (Fennell, 1998). Ecotourism often takes place in protected and remote regions, areas of exceptional beauty, ecological interest and cultural importance (Wearing and Neil, 1999), but ecotourism can also take place in human made places (Fennell, 2013). Wallace and Pierce (1996) provide an overview of the fundamental structure of ecotourism. They suggest that ecotourism:

- Minimizes impacts;
- Increases awareness;
- Contributes to conservation;
- Allows local people to make their own decisions;
- Directs economic benefits to local people; and
- Provides opportunities for local people to enjoy natural areas.

This overview comprises conservation, which implies a direct link to biodiversity. Ecotourism definitions often imply linking to biodiversity e.g., conservation, enjoy natural areas, ecological connections, etc., that are not often explicit and thus, the word "biodiversity" is not used directly when defining ecotourism. However, most definitions imply that biodiversity is one of ecotourism's core ideas. In ecotourism, there continues to be a strong and a prevailing element of cultural relativism. Consequently, what qualifies as ecotourism in some regions or countries does not necessarily hold true in others (Fennell, 2001).

Colombia's protected areas system began in the 1950s with the establishment of seven forest reserves. In the 1960s the first National Park, namely, Cueva de Los Guacharos was founded between the states of Huila and Caquetá (Serrano, 2011). Colombia's National Parks offer great opportunities for ecotourism. Currently, there are 58 protected areas. These include National Parks, Flora and Fauna Sanctuaries (Santuarios de Flora y Fauna) and smaller parks (Via Parque) (Parques Nacionales de Colombia, 2014) (Table 1 and Figure 2).

National Parks offer *ecotourism based activities* such as bird watching, trekking, canoeing, high mountain activities, water sports, snorkeling, scuba diving, photography and contact with indigenous cultures. However, some of these activities fall into other types of tourism, e.g., adventure tourism and need to be better designed and focused within the philosophical and theoretical background of ecotourism.

Commonly the idea of visiting a National Park within the context of ecotourism is often mistaken by other tourism types. Moreover, some tourist stakeholders are only interesting in selling *tours* and pay little attention to what is being sold. Despite the dangerous and socially unstable places, there are locations in Colombia that are safe, but are not well known where ecotourism can be practiced.

Table 1. Colombia's National Protected Areas

National Park	Nature Reserve	Unique Natural Area	Flora Sanctuary	Fauna Sanctuary	Flora and Fauna Sanctuary	Via Park
Amazon Region						
Yaigojé Apaporis	Puinawai		Orito Ingi - Ande			
Serranía de los Churumbelos	Nukak					
Río Puré						
La Paya						
Cahuinarí						
Alto Fragua Indi Wasi						
Nukak						
Amacayacu						
Serranía de Chiribiquete						
Northeast Andes Region						
Tamá		Los Estoraques			Iguaque	
Serranía de Los Yariguíes					Guanentá Alto Río Fonce	
Pisba						
Catatumbo Barí						
Cocuy						
Western Andes Region						
Tatamá					Otún Quimbaya	
Selva de Florencia					Isla de la Corota	
Nevado del Huila					Galeras	
Las Orquídeas						
Complejo Volcanico Doña Juana - Cascabel						
Las Hermosas						
Puracé						
Los Nevados						
Cueva de los Guácharos						

Table 1. (Continued)

National Park	Nature Reserve	Unique Natural Area	Flora Sanctuary	Fauna Sanctuary	Flora and Fauna Sanctuary	Via Park
Caribbean Region						
Corales de Profundidad				Acandí, Playón y Playona	Los Colorados	Isla de Salamanca
Ciénaga Grande de Santa Marta					El Corchal "El Mono Hernández"	
Paramillo					Los Flamencos	
Sierra Nevada de Santa Marta						
Old Providence McBean Lagoon						
Macuira						
Corales del Rosario y de San Bernardo						
Tayrona						
Orinoco Region						
Chingaza						
Sierra de la Macarena						
Cordillera de Los Picachos						
El Tuparro						
Tinigua						
Sumapaz						
Pacific Region						
Utría					Malpelo	
Uramba Bahía Málaga						
Sanquianga						
Munchique						
Los Katíos						
Farallones de Cali						
Gorgona						

Source: Parques Nacionales de Colombia 2014.

CULTURAL ASPECTS

Currently, Colombia is a cultural rich country. Social groups can be traced back to the early indigenous groups that thrived during prehistoric times and early cultures found at the time of the Spanish conquest in the 1500s. Beginning in the early 1500s, for three centuries, Spanish conquerors devastated Colombia's indigenous peoples and their cultures through brute force, slaughtering them, enslaving them, and forcing them to work in mines or *encomiendas,* estates granted by the crown to Spanish administrators (Bouvier, 2009). It is believed that when the Spaniards arrived, between 6 to 10 million indigenous peoples inhabited what today is known as Colombia (Bouvier, 2009). Many of these indigenous cultures have disappeared as a consequence of violence and mixing processes. The 1991 constitution evinced recognition of Colombian ethnic minorities in measures to promote their participation in the political system, though indigenous and ethnic congressional groups, and by acknowledging their cultural and territorial rights (Hudson, 2010). Colombia ratified International Labor Organization (ILO) Conventions 107 (1957) and 169 (1989) on Indigenous and Tribal Peoples and has applied these treaties in a systematic manner to develop legal instruments for the protection of the rights of peoples and communities (Davies and Sánchez, 2003). Thus, Colombia's ethnic groups have increased their political and social participation, and they have explored new forms of collaborative action (Hudson, 2010). Currently, Colombia's national population includes about 80 indigenous groups located throughout the country and a large number of Afro-Colombian communities, many of which inhabit the Atlantic and Pacific coastal regions and the islands of San Andrés, Providencia and Santa Catalina (Hudson, 2010). Indigenous peoples, comprise approximately 3.4% of the total population and Afro-Colombians 10.5% (Hudson, 2010). The indigenous population is of particular importance in the jungle biomes and natural savannahs of the Amazon and Orinoco, and on the Guajira peninsula and on the northeast of the Cauca state (Davies and Sánchez, 2003).

Several arguments suggest that the development of indigenous communities is compatible with ecotourism (Coria and Calfucura, 2011). First, there is a significant overlap between ecotourism and the development of indigenous communities in the sense that the world's least developed areas which are usually the most natural coincide with the traditional homelands of indigenous people (Fisher and Treg, 2007; Coria and Calfucura, 2011). Second, ecotourists generally have an explicit desire to have a positive impact, i.e., to patronize local services and respect the customs of the destination hosts

(West and Carrier, 2004; Coria and Calfucura, 2011). The ecotourism literature is full of examples characterizing indigenous people as wise protectors of the land, with accompanying inferences about how non-indigenous people might begin to live more in harmony with the environment – in the manner of traditional societies (Fennell, 2008b). There may be serious philosophical and operational problems inherent in packaging aboriginal ecotourism as having a superior environmental ethic, and a need for further research and changed management practices (Fennell, 2008b). Besides protecting biodiversity, ecotourism in indigenous communities is meant to improve the livelihood of the members of the community (Coria and Calfucura, 2011). However, several authors have argued that many indigenous ecotourism ventures had not had a significant effect on local livelihoods and in fact any negative effects on biodiversity (Kiss, 2004). The implementation of ecotourism ventures by indigenous communities is not the exemption, and it does not automatically imply conservation or economic development for these groups (Coria and Calfucura, 2011). There are many examples of projects that produce revenues for local communities and improve local attitudes towards conservation, but the contribution of community-based ecotourism to conservation and local economic development is limited by factors such as smaller areas and few people involved, limited earnings, weak linkages between biodiversity gains and commercial success, and the competitive and specialized nature of the tourism industry (Kiss, 2004).

Colombia has a great potential for integrating ecotourism activities and indigenous groups. Building initiatives that promote community ecotourism could benefit local communities and the maintenance of native cultures. However, in the Tayrona National Park, Ojeda (2012) found that environmental protection discourses and practices have translated into land-grabbing mechanisms under which the protection of nature, allegedly made possible by its commodification for tourist consumption justifies and even legitimates the disposition of local community members such as fishermen, transporters and peasants (Ojeda, 2012). Under the cited circumstances, ecotourism is used as a pretext for other purposes and clearly loses its focus and philosophical basis. Moreover, Ojeda (2012) reported that a group of local community members, peasants, in Tayrona's buffer zone have been produced as eco-guardians through their participation in the project Posadas Turísticas (Tourist Lodges), a development project that uses ecotourism as a means for illicit crop eradication, environmental conservation, community building and peacemaking. Project participants had the commitment to maintain the land „clean" (coca-free) and to devote it to conservation and sustainable economic activities such as organic small-scale farming (coffee, cacao and tropical fruits), beekeeping and ecotourism (Ojeda, 2012). However, some of these peasants were foreigners with an obscure background, i.e., cocaleros (coca growers and pickers) that came into the zone looking for possible job opportunities. This scenario provides a background of conflict related issues that have occurred in the Tayrona National Park. Moreover, Ojeda (2012) points out that ecotourism''s broken promises of conservation, development and peacemaking have been insufficient to generate viable livelihood strategies and more inclusive politics that could lead to the region''s transformation. It is in that sense that tourism-based conservation in the Tayrona area has made of ecotourism a powerful strategy of accumulation by dispossession, complementing other mechanisms of land grabbing in the country (Ojeda, 2012). The ecotourism sector in other Colombian National Parks lacks comprehensive investigations and there is little governmental presence. Ecotourism has the potential to improve indigenous communities'' livelihood possibilities, in practice the distribution of economic benefits is very uneven and tends to favor stakeholders outside the protected area and/or the involved communities'' elites (Coria and Calfucura, 2012). Exploitation, cultural erosion, indigenous rights, land agreements, prior informed consent to access to indigenous lands, intellectual property (authentic handicrafts), failing rural development initiatives and so on, are all threats that need to be addressed, especially in ecotourism (Fennell, 2008b).

ECOTOURISM RESEARCH IN COLOMBIA

The history of environmental institutions in Colombia dates back to 1968 with the establishment of INDERENA (Instituto Nacional de Recursos Naturales), that later on (1993) became the Ministry of Environment (Ministrio del Medio Ambiente) and then, in 2002 became the Ministry of Environment, Housing and Territorial Development (Ministerio de Ambiente, Vivienda y Desarrollo Territorial) (Sierra, 2011). Currently, this institution is the Ministry of Environment and Sustainable Development (Ministerio de Ambiente y Desarrollo Sostenible).

The origin of ecotourism in Colombia has been difficult to trace in the past due to the lack of information. However, the first attempt to consolidate an ecotourism program occurred in the early 1980s, when President Belosario Betancour created the first environmental agencies such as INDERENA that administered Colombia''s National Parks. After Betancour''s mandate,

President Virgilio Barco consolidated the first visiting centers within National Parks (Jimenez, 2010).

Most of the published research has been at the local level in Journals and Books. Few information has been published in international journals and or books. Most investigations in the field have been carried on ecotourism in the Andes comprising Cundinamarca and Boyacá States. The government through the Tourism Ministry (Ministerio de Industria y Turismo) has produced a series of book guides on nature tourism. However, these guides are only offered to a particular economic segment of the population and cannot be purchased by low income individuals.

Ecotourism research has been conducted in several areas in Colombia. This is evidenced by works conducted in the Amazon (Fraguell et al., 2003; Sierra, 2011; Ochoa et al., 2013); Atlantic Coast focusing on conflict-related dynamics and ecotourism in the Tayrona National Park (Ojeda, 2012) and promising animal and plant species for ecotourism in Sucre state (Sampedro-M et al., 2013); The Andes, focusing on the development of an ecotourism network (Vásquez et al., 2010), building a comprehensive framework for ecotourism and wetland restoration for Bogotá's urban wetlands (Ramírez and Fennell 2015 in press). Other works have focused on general aspects of ecotourism in Colombia (Ospina et al., 2013).

Ecotourism in the Amazon region of Colombia has focused on lineal field excursions though the Amazon (Fraguell et al., 2003). However, due to the fact the few reliable information is available, the current status of ecotourism in the Amazon possibly has a different picture. On 2003, The Colombian Amazon was not an important ecotourism destination for international travelers (Fraguell et al., 2003). However, at the local, national level, the Amazon region of Colombia basin attracted numerous ecotourists (Fraguell et al., 2003). Unfortunately these authors do not provide the number of ecotourists visiting the Amazon region of Colombia near Leticia the capital city of Amazonas State, Colombia. Due to the fact that the ecotourism sector is not well developed, the tourism industry has filled the gap with field guided excursion activities, various trekking activities. For example, in Amacayacu National Park, visitors are offered short one day trips or longer ones. Activities include field-guided tours by native indigenous guides such as La Ceiba trail, canopy trail, field tours (walking) though the jungle, animal observation, and indigenous community visits (Fraguell et al., 2003). Ochoa et al. (2013) studied the local community vison on derived benefits form ecotourism in Amacayacu National Park. The study documented the community's perception through a series of enquires. These investigators found that ecotourism generates economic revenues but impacts livehoods and the local culture. The local community's consensus feels there is no derived benefit form ecotourism mainly because the Amacayacu's concession sets unbalanced rules where the local community does not benefit at all. The concession model offers a controversial view where the local community's benefits are underestimated.

In the Andes region of Colombia, Vásquez et al. (2010) proposed the creation of a local network for ecotourism for some localities within Cundinamarca and Boyacá States. This network seeks to develop an ecotourism definition based on opinions form stakeholders, ecotourists, the local community, local governmental organizations. The outcome of this work was a proposal for an ecotourism network wherein ecotourism attractions are linked to the ecotourism stakeholders (Vásquez et al., 2010).

Other works in the Andes have focused on developing an ecotourism framework for wetlands. Ramírez and Fennell (2015) proposed a framework for optimizing the use of Bogotá's wetlands through ecotourism. Bogotá's wetlands are localized on the eastern cordillera of the Andes on a vast savannah. Within this great savannah lies Bogotá, the capital city of Colombia, which is a wetland-rich city (Ramírez et al., 2013). Bogota is home to 14 wetlands that face current environmental problems because of human intervention. These wetlands are among the most remarkable places due to the rich biodiversity and cultural Heritance they harbor (Ramírez and Fennell, 2015). The framework is divided into four components. The first component is based on a potential method for optimizing suitable use of wetlands by industry based on the considerations outlined by Wang et al. (2008); the second component includes the seven dimensions of STEEPLE (an acronym for Political, Economic, Social, Technological, and Environmental analysis, and involves the many broad considerations that affect the tourism industry environment, e.g., the political environment, and which are outside the control of the service provider; the third includes industry considerations with a specific focus on ecotourism; and the fourth touches briefly on an integrated wetland use and protection plan. Within this context, the word "wetland industry" refers to a series of industries, which take advantage of wetland resources or ecosystem services to produce products or provide services for humans (Wang et al., 2008). Industries such as wetland planting, wetland aquaculture, wetland tourism, and wetland sewage treatment, are all included in the category of wetland industry (Wang et al., 2008). Alongside the industries we include wetland ecotourism, wetland management, wetland restoration and wetland conservation (Ramírez and Fennell, 2015). The proposed framework, therefore, acts as a tool for wetland conservation.

Bogotá, not unlike many cities in the developing world, has suffered from many of the problems identified by Wang et al. (2008). Identifying and addressing these problems through the development of such a framework may prove helpful in stimulating local, national, and international cooperation for economic growth, education, and conservation (Ramírez and Fennell, 2015).

Furthermore, research in the Andes has focused on teaching ecotourism in Bogotá's wetlands. Ramírez and Davenport (2015) proposed the basic information for teaching an ecotourism class is based on six wetland-related aspects 1) infrastructure for ecotourism, 2) biodiversity, 3) cultural aspects, e.g., wetland history 3) wetland management issues 4) environmental issues and 5) conservation and restoration 6) community involvement. These key aspects were analyzed with students in three different wetlands; Santa María del Lago, Córdoba and Guaymaral. None of the wetlands has developed a reliable ecotourism program. The comparison of management, restoration, conservation, environmental issues and community involvement among wetlands provided an interesting opportunity to determine ecotourism attributes and possibilities for developing ecotourism (Ramírez and Davenport, 2015).

Ecotourism studies in the Atlantic Coast have focused on ecotourism, neoliberal conservation and land grabbing in the Tayrona National Natural Park, Colombia (Ojeda, 2012). This work examines how ecotourism complements this land-grabbing logic despite green imperatives of environmental conservation and tourism „done right" (Ojeda, 2012). This investigation proposes that ecotourism has been used as a *pretext* to conduct licit actions under a roughly illicit background of drugs, paramilitary and related groups.

POLICY

The policy surrounding ecotourism in Colombia has been considered greatly controversial due to the fact that many of the laws and decrees passed remain in paper and actions are lacking. Ecotourism in Colombia is supporting the General Law of Tourism (Law 300 of 1996 articles 26-30) (Ley General de Turismo, 1996). This law establishes in article 26 a definition for ecotourism. Article 27 focuses on jurisdiction and competence. Article 28, deal with ecotourism planning, especially in National Parks. Article 29, focuses on the promotion of ecotourism by Colombia's government. Article 30 focuses on governmental coordination for ecotourism programs by the Ministry of Economic Development (Ministerio de Desarrollo Económico) and the Ministry of Environmental Affairs (Ministreio del Medio Ambiente). Other governmental documents include the Policy for ecotourism development generated in 2003 (Ministerio de Comercio, Industria y Turismo, 2003) and the guidelines for community based ecotourism in 2006 (Ministerio de Ambiente, Vivienda y Desarrollo Territorial, 2006). However, these guidelines remain in paper and are not conducive to *real* actions.

One of the most controversial measures adopted by Colombia''s government were *concessions* or treaties between Colombia''s National Park System (Parques Nacionales Naturales de Colombia) and organizations from the private sector. Concessions were established since 2005 within the policy guidelines of the document CONPES 3296 of 2004 *Guidelines for private participation in on ecotourism services in Colombia's National Natural Parks* (SSNA, 2014). These concessions provided administrative and jurisdictional control to private organizations over several National Parks and protected areas (Table 2). The use of national areas was then regulated by *private owners* that would develop tourism and ecotourism to obtain large economic revenues. The controversy was generated when green pretexts were mixed with political and excluding issues. For example, the Tayrona National Park was practically *privatized* by a concession (Ojeda, 2012). Also, some of the so called ecotourism activities and packages were not within the philosophy of real ecotourism. Some concessions i.e., Los Nevados and Amacayacu have been liquidated and is the process of being liquidated respectively, due to natural disasters affecting these National Parks. Amacayacu''s concession is in the process of being terminated because of flooding of the Visitor''s Center Yewaé by the Amazon River in 2012. Also, possible landslides studies determined the censure of ecotourism activities in 2012. However, Sierra (2011) proposes that the Amacayacu concession provided consistent measures for reducing human impacts and changed the illicit structure by providing other work options. Furthermore, the concession model of Amacayacu National Park, hastened economic development which causes non-steady conditions for the indigenous groups inhabit this National Park (Sierra, 2011). In los Nevados National Park, the concession was liquidated after evaluating the risk of a possible volcanic eruption of El Ruiz Volcano in 2012.

Table 2. Concessions of National Parks since 2005

State (s)	National Park / Santuary	Concession (Private Sector)
Amazonas	Amacayacú*	Aviatur (50%), Hoteles Decameron Colombia (35%) and Cielos Abiertos (15%)
Magdalena	Tayrona	Aviatur (98%), Camara de Comercio de Santa Marta (1%) and Passarola Tours (1%)
Cauca	Gorgona	Aviatur (95%) and Avia Caribbean (5%)
Tolima, Quindio, Risaralda y Caldas	Los Nevados*	Caja de compensación Familiar Caldas (30%), Instituto de Financiamiento Promoción y Desarrollo de Manizales (10%), Instituto de Financiaminto Promoción y Desarrollo de Caldas (20%) and Aviatur (30%) and Sociedad Hotelera de Caldas (10%)
Risaralda	Otún Quimbaya Flora and Fauna Sanctuary	Unión Temporal Concesión Gorgona
Magdalena	Salamanca Island Vía Park	Corporación Bioparque

* Denote concession liquidated or in the process of being liquidated by 2014.

EDUCATION

Based on ideological and philosophical perspectives we have developed in this chapter, it is important to find the motivation and the arguments to assume new life attitudes towards nature and what we call ecotourism. From this reality, to know the world, enjoy the landscape should awaken in us the ethical sensibility, as well as the emotional sensibility providing a sublime meaning or a high one, that represents nature in our lives and this is only accomplished if we self-educate in ecotourism. To self-educate is to assume by one"s self the responsibility to face difficulties in life with the reality of one"s experience, i.e., the new knowledge acquired turns into one"s ideal, experiential aspirations, that taken to practice, have heart and soul. To be ecologically educated, is to understand that, if, as an individual one does not protect natural places where one"s lives because of lack consciousness, one will cause the destruction of the place. From here, the sacred sense is understood, that the natives of each region of the world, vitally understood, they sensed the occult mystery of nature, they were identified by it, respected it and were willing to give their lives for it because they knew it was life itself. Traditionally, it is known the Chibchas, a pre-Hispanic community that inhabited the valleys of Sogamoso, Villa de Leyva, Duitama and Bogotá"s savannah worshipped the Sun god (Rodíguez, 2011). This meant a profound respect for life, because without the Sun there is no possible agriculture. Their planting sites for agriculture were sacred places. First, because it guarantees life and second because it encloses a mystery. This is why the indigenous people did not allow foreign or external people from their culture to visit crop planting or water sources. To step on a crop planting or move the muddy waters of a lake caused a negative influence by damaging the site. Thus, these places were considered sacred and sacred is what we should pass on to our children. Ecotourism has the mission to educate adults and children, but also the government and institutions.

ECOTOURISM AND CONFLICTS

Situated in tropical South America, Colombia has a great diversity of culture, heritage, landscapes and areas of high ecological interest, but it is also embroiled in ongoing armed conflict between the government, paramilitary groups, guerilla groups and drug cartels (Ospina, 2006).

The high level of political instability and corruption has led to a series of social issued that date back to colonial times. Over the years, many regions have been under the siege of insurgent groups such as guerrilla paramilitary and norcotrafic related illicit forces. This has created severe social an economic problems that negatively impact the tourism industry. For example, in Colombia, the Purace National Park in the south of the country consists of volcanic landscapes and thermal waters that allow for the observation of diverse wildlife, immersion in thermal waters, and long walks (Williams et al., 2001). However, the social instability, political problems and the violence associated with drugs have inhibited Colombia in its development of tourism and, as a result, the Purace National Park has not been able to realize its potential and benefit from a healthy flow of ecotourists (Leitch, 1993; Williams et al., 2001). Similarly, the Tayrona National Park is marked by the strong presence of both official and irregular (i.e., Guerrilla and Paramilitary) armed forces (Ojeda, 2012). The illicit presence is due to the fact that Tayrona is connected to the Sierra Nevada de Santa Marta, where mostly illegal crops (marihuana, coca and poppies) are harvested and shipped to Central America and Mexico, to then be sent to their final destinations in the U.S. and Europe (Ojeda, 2012). Ecotourism programs associated with the presence of huge extensions of *M. flexuosa* palm swamps (cananguchales) have been conducted in Caquetá State, which is located in the upper basin of the Orteguaza River, at the Amazonian Piedmont to the Northwest of the Amazon Basin in Colombia (Ricaurte et al., 2014). A few years ago, these sites were regularly visited during weekends for leisure activity and for the multiple use of this plant. However, due to armed conflicts in the region, ecotourism currently has decreased, as safety cannot be warranted (Ricaurte et al., 2014). Although, that the armed conflict occurred in many places, currently there are many locations in Colombia, where the conflict has been resolved and such places can now be visited without any risk. For example, Villavicencio, on the llanos region, and the Boyacá state in Cundinamarca among other regions.

CONCLUSION

The field of ecotourism in Colombia needs to be better defined under a philosophical lens. Colombia has a number of developmental possibilities for the field of ecotourism. Colombia's rich biodiversity and cultural heritage are the main attractive elements the ecotourism can explore. Under the current political and social conditions, the county faces difficult times for developing a consistent ecotourism sector efficiently and systematically managed by different sectors such as, the public, private and nongovernmental organizations as well as volunteer programs. Colombia's National Parks have a great potential for establishing ecotourism programs. However, under the current governmental management, these unique places have been almost forgotten, many of them facing serious violence and social related conflicts that are counterproductive for the tourism and ecotourism sectors. Education and philosophy are core areas for the understanding and unraveling intricate ecological perspectives that surround ecotourism in Colombia. In conclusion, the invitation is to assume ecology as a way of life, because there is a need to *do ecology* not natural biology but also of human nature.

Today, it is a requirement to provide formative and informative orientation to facilitate the urgent comprehension of the required measures to protect the environment. Moreover, the ecotourism potential in Colombia is enormous due to territorial vastness and that conflict-related zones are small in proportion to the amount of territory. It is necessary that the world breaks the multiple prejudges and ideas generated by ill-intentioned persons that have discredited Colombia's rich and singular tourism world.

REFERENCES

Aristotles., (1999). *Retorica.* Editorial Gredos, Madrid.

Bookbinder, M. P., Dinerstein, E., Rijal, A., Cauley, H., 1998. Ecotourism's support of biodiversity conservation. *Conservation Biology* 12 (6), 1399-1404.

Boo, E. (1990). *Ecotourism: The Potentials and Pitfalls* (Vols 1 & 2). Washington, DC: World Wide Fund for Nature.

Bouvier, V., (2009) *Colombia: Building peace in a war time.* U. S. Institute of Peace Press, Washington.

Budowski, G., 1976. Tourism and environmental conservation: conflict, coexistence or symbiosis? *Environmental Conservation* 3, 27-31.

Cavallé, M., 2006. *La sabiduría recobrada.* Ediciones Martínez Roca, Madrid.

Calderón-Sáenz E. (Ed.). 2006. *Libro Rojo de Plantas de Colombia.* Volumen 3: Orquídeas, Primera Parte. Serie Libros Rojos de Especies Amenazadas de Colombia. Bogotá, Colombia. Instituto Alexander von Humboldt - Ministerio de Ambiente, Vivienda y Desarrollo Territorial. 828p.

Coria, J. and Calfucura, E. (2011). Ecotourism and the development of indigenous communities: The good, the bad, and the ugly. *Ecological Economics* 73, 47-55.

Davies, S. and Sánchez, E. (2003) *Indigenous peoples and Afro-Colombian communities*. In: Giugale, M. M., Lafourcade, O. and Luff, C. (Eds.). Colombia: the economic foundation of peace. The International Bank of Reconstruction and Development/the World Bank, Washington, D. C. p. 787-823.

Donegan T., Quevedo A., McMullan M., & Salaman P. 2011. *Revision of the status of bird species occurring or reported in Colombia 2011.* Conservación Colombiana 15: 4-21

Fennell D. A. (1998) „Ecotourism in Canada", *Annals of Tourism Research* 25, 231-234.

Fennell D. A. (2001). A Content Analysis of Ecotourism Definitions, *Current Issues in Tourism,* 4, 403-421.

Fennell, D. A. (2008a) *Ecotourism.* Third Edition. Routledge. New York.

Fennell D. A. (2008b) Ecotourism and the myth of indigenous stewardship. *Journal of Sustainable Tourism* 16, 129-149.

Fennell D. A. (2013). Contesting the zoo as a setting for ecotourism, and the design of a first principle, *Journal of Ecotourism,* 12, 1-14.

Fisher, B. and Treg, C. (2007). Poverty and biodiversity: measuring the overlap of human poverty and the biodiversity hotspots. *Ecological Economics* 61, 93-101.

Fraguell, M. R. y Muñoz, J. C. (2003). Ecoturismo itinerante en el Trapecio Amazónico. *Estudios y Perspectivasen Turismo* 12, 48-62.

Gentry, A., (1986) Species richness and floristic composition of Choco region plant communities. *Caldasia* 15, 71-75.

Gössling, S. (1999). Ecotourism: a means to safeguard biodiversity and ecosystem functions? *Ecological Economics* 29, 303-320.

Hudson, R. A. (2010). *Colombia: A country study.* Fifth Edition. Federal Research Division Library of Congress (U.S.), Washington.

Jiménez, L. H. (2010) *Ecoturismo: Oferta y desarrollo sistémico regional.* Bogotá: Ecoe Ediciones, Bogotá.

Ley General de Turismo, 1996. *Ley general de turismo.* Colombia. http://www.mincit.gov.co/descargar.php?idFile = 2294Accessed 30 Sep 2014.

Jørgensen, P. M., Ulloa-Ulloa, C., León, B., León-Yánez, S., Beck, S. G., Nee, M., Zarucchi, J. L., Celis, M., Bernal R. and Gradstein. R. (2011). *Regional patterns of vascular plant diversity and endemism.* In: Climate change and biodiversity in the Tropical Andes, Herzog, S. K., Martínez, R., Jørgensen P. M. and Tiess H. (Eds.). Inter-American Institute for Global Change Research (IAI) and Scientific Committee on Problems of the Environment (SCOPE). p. 192-203

Kiss, A. (2004). Is community-based ecotourism a good use of biodiversity conservation funding? *Trends in Ecology & Evolution* 19, 232-237.

Leitch, W. (1993) *Parques Nacionales de Sudamérica.* Guía Para el Visitante. EmecéEditores, Buenos Aires.

Malloy, D. C. and Fennell, D. A. (1998a). Ecotourism and ethics: moral development and organizational cultures, *Journal of Travel Research* 36, 47-56.

Ministerio de Comercio, Industria y Turismo, 2003. *Política para el desarrollo del ecoturismo.* Colombia, 58 p.

Ministerio de Comercio, Industria y Turismo 2012. *Guía de turismo de naturaleza.* Colombia: Panamericana Formas e Impresos S. A. 420 p.

Milton Ricardo Ospina, M. R., Mora, R. and Romero, J. A. Ecoturismo: diagnóstico y propuesta estratégica para la oferta de destinos ecoturísticos en Colombia por parte de las agencias de turismo localizadas en Bogotá, D. C. *Cuadernos Latinoamericanos de Administración.* 9: 7-28.

Nowaczek, A. M., Moran-Cahusac, C. and Fennel, D. A., (2007). *Against the current: Striving for ethical ecotourism.* In: Higham, J. (Ed.). Critical issues in ecotourism: understanding a complex tourism phenomenon. Elsevier. Oxford. pp. 136-157.

Ochoa, F. A., James, J. y Márquez, G. (2013). Visión comunitaria de los beneficios derivados del ecoturismo en el Parque Nacional Amacayacú (Amazonas Colombia). *Gestión y Ambiente.* 16, 17-32.

Ojeda, D. (2012). Green pretexts: Ecotourism, neoliberal conservation and land grabbing in Tayrona National Natural Park, Colombia. *Journal of Peasant Studies.* 39, 357-375.

Ospina, G. A. (2006). War and ecotourism in the National Parks of Colombia: some reflections on the public risk and adventure. *Internacional Journal of Tourism Research* 8, 241-246.

Parques Nacionales de Colombia. *Ecoturismo en los parques nacionales de Colombia.* http://www.parquesnacionales.gov.co/portal/sistema-de-parques-nacionales-naturales/Documento consultado Septiembre 2014.

Plotino. (1985). *Enéadas:* Libros III y IV. Madrid: Editorial Gredos.

Ramírez, F., Davenport, T. L. and Kallarackal, J. (2013). *Bogotá's urban wetlands.* In: Lavigne, G. and Cote, C. Colombia social, economic and environmental issues. Nova Publishers, New York, p 1-80.

Ramírez, F., and Davenport, T. L., (2014). Class time: teaching ecotourism to undergraduate students using Bogotá's urban wetlands as a model. *Journal of Ecotourism* (In Press).

Ramírez, F. and Davenport, T. L. (2013). *Elasmobranchs from marine and freshwater environments in Colombia:* A review. In: Lavigne, G. and Cote, C. Colombia social, economic and environmental issues. Nova Publishers, New York, p 81-128.

Ramírez, F. and Davenport, T. L. (2015). *Dietary-morphological relationships of nineteen fish species from an Amazonian blackwater stream in Colombia.* Limnologica (in press)

Ramírez, F. and Fennell, D. A. (2015). A comprehensive framework for ecotourism and wetland restoration: The case of Bogotá, Colombia. *Journal of Ecotourism.* (In Press)

Rodríguez, J. V., 2011. *Los chibchas: Hijos del sol, la luna y los Andes: orígenes de su diversidad.* Editorial Universidad Nacional de Colombia (Sede Bogotá), Bogotà

Ricaurte, L. F., Wantzen, K. M., Agudelo, E., Betancourt, B., Jukka, J. (2014). Participatory rural appraisal of ecosystem services of wetlands in the Amazonian Piedmont of Colombia: elements for a sustainable management concept. *Wetlands Ecology and Management* 22, 343-361.

Saenz, S., Walschburger, T., González, J C., León, J. McKenney, B. and Kiesecker, J. (2013). A framework for implementing and valuing biodiversity offsets in Colombia: A landscape scale perspective. *Sustainability* 5, 4961-4987.

Sampedro-M, A., Álvarez-P, A., Domínguez, L. M., Herrera-M, I. (2013). *Especies promisorias para el ecoturismo en "Campo Aventura Roca Madre",* Toluviejo-Sucre, Colombia. *Revista MVZ Córdoba* 18, 3387-3398.

SIB. (2014). Sistema de Información sobre Biodiversidad de Colombia. Las cifras de biodiversidad en Colombia. http://www.sibcolombia. net/web/ sib/cifras. Accessed 10 Mar 2013.

Sierra, M. (2011) L'évolution des politiques de protection et l'intégration du secteur privé dans la conservation: L'exemple du Parc amazonien Amacayacu en Colombie et l'application du nouveau système de gestión: Concession. CM.H.LB. *Caravelle* 96, 111-132.

SSNA. (2014). *Concesión de servicios ecoturísticos.* Parques Naturales Nacionales de Colombia. http://www.parquesnacionales.gov. co/PNN/portel/libreria/php/decide.php?patron = 01.022114 Accessed 30 Sep 2014.

Vásquez, J. A., Posada, A. y Laytón, P. (2010). Perspectiva del ecoturismo en el Altiplano Cundiboyacense para conformar una red local. *Revista U. D. C. A Actividades & Divulgación Científica.* 13, 147-156.

Wang, Y., Yao, Y., and Ju, M. (2008). Wise use of wetlands: current state of protection and utilization of Chinese wetlands and recommendations for improvement. *Environmental Management* 41, 793-808.

Williams, P. W., Singh, T. V., and Schlüter, R. (2001). *Mountain ecotourism: Creating a sustainable future.* In: Encyclopedia of ecotourism. Weaver, D. B. (Ed.). CABI publishing. Wallingford, p. 205-218.

WCMC (World Conservation Monitoring Centre), 1992. *Global Biodiversity: Status of the Earth's Living Resources.* Chapman and Hall, London A report compiled by the World Conservation Monitoring Centre.

Wearing, S. and Neil, J. (1999), *Ecotourism: Impacts, potentials and possibilities.* Reed Educational and Professional Publishing Ltd. Boston.

West, P. and Carrier, J. (2004). Ecotourism and authenticity: getting away from it all? *Current Anthropology* 45, 483-498.

In: Ecotourism
Editor: Shannon C. Brophy
ISBN: 978-1-63482-027-1
© 2015 Nova Science Publishers, Inc.

Chapter 5

ACCOUNTING FOR THE UNDERWATER BEHAVIOUR OF HONG KONG DIVERS

Shan-shan Chung

Department of Biology, Hong Kong Baptist University
Hong Kong

ABSTRACT

Studies have found that marine tourists can cause impact to the underwater environment by breaking corals and disturbing coral-associated benthic organisms. However, which type of dive tourists inflicts the most harm on the marine ecosystem? Few studies are able to throw light into this.

Making use of data from the direct observation of diving behaviour and self-reported findings on the environmental attitudes and values of 80 Hong Kong divers, this chapter brings to light factors or attributes that would affect or associate with divers" underwater behaviour. It was found that by carrying a camera, divers made 9.8 more intended contacts per dive.

Divers who are not so willing to avoid using non-biodegradable shampoos (a pro-environment behaviour) would also make more contacts on the marine biota. However, even the more disciplined divers in the sample are not so willing to financially contribute to marine conservation. On the whole, attitudinal and value-based variables can only explain about 20% of the variations in their underwater behaviour. Given existing findings, it is advisable to the underwater tourism industry to not just

educate but also impose dive guide intervention to reduce divers"
intended contacts on marine biota to protect the already stressful
underwater environment.

Keywords: Scuba diving, intentional contacts, marine biota, diving tourism,
ownership variable, empowerment variable

INTRODUCTION

Being a non-consumptive use of the marine environment, scuba
diving is generally thought to be compatible with the principles of
resource sustainability because the sustainability of such activity is
predicated on the continued existence of underwater attractions. Yet, with
the increase in the popularity of scuba diving and nature-based tourism
(Guzner, Novplansky, Shalit, & Chadwick, 2010), there are reasons to
believe that dive tourism may be stressing the marine environment not
just in world-known dive sites, such as Sipadan and Palau, but also other
less famous regional or even local sites, e.g., Sodwana Bay of South
Africa (Lucrezi, Saayman & van der Merwe, 2013). Hong Kong is
situated in the sub-tropical region with warm climate throughout the year.
While summer months are the peak seasons for scuba diving activities,
with suitable exposure protection, diving is possible even in cooler
months.

However, is scuba diving really an activity that is fully compatible
with environmental conservation goals? Studies have concluded that
recreational divers can cause damages to corals and coral-associated
benthic organisms by breaking coral skeletons or abrading their tissues
(Hawkins & Roberts, 1992; Smith, Scarr, & Scarpaci, 2010).

The damage caused by individual divers and anchoring of dive boats
can range from minor (Walters & Samways, 2001; Zakai & Chadwick-
Furman, 2002) to serious localized decline in coral cover (Hawkins,
Roberts, van't Hof, de Meyer, Tratalos, & Aldam, 1999). Mis-behaved
marine tourists can also cause surprisingly devastating damage, such as
destroying 72 kg of living coral in a single incident (Woodland &
Hooper, 1977).

Diving also inevitably increases sediment resuspension and may
adversely impact sessile organisms (di Franco, Milazzo, Baiata,
Tomasello, & Chemello, 2009). As a result, environmental damage
caused by tourists, including divers, is a concern that parallel similar
damage in terrestrial areas.

FACTORS AFFECTING DIVERS' UNDERWATER BEHAVIOUR

Thapa, Graefe, & Meyer (2006) discovered that the level of recreational specialization was positively correlated with divers" environmental friendliness attitude and there was negative correlation between the number of logged dives and the number of contacts on corals (Worachananant, Carter, Hockings, & Reopanichkul, 2008). This relationship between diving experience or skills and the number of contacts divers made underwater is not necessarily universal (Barker 2003; Chung, Au & Qiu, 2013; di Franco et al. 2009). Demographic characteristics of the divers, such as gender and education level are also relevant. Chung et al. (2013) found that better educated divers will behave better underwater, a finding that concurs with the phenomenon that more educated people are more likely to engage in pro-environmental behaviour (Jones & Dunlap, 1992; Scott & Willits, 1994). Worachananant et al. (2008) found that female divers tended to cause more damage than male divers. This however goes against the general environmental behaviourial research findings that females are more likely to engage in some if not all pro-environmental behaviour for cultural and social-structural reasons (Chen, Peterson, Hull, Lu, Lee, Hong, & Liu, 2011; Hunter, Hatch, & Johnson, 2004; Stern, Dietz, & Kalof, 1993) and is also different from that concluded by Rouphael & Inglis (2001) who studied 214 female and male divers visiting the Great Barrier Reef in 1994. Rouphael & Inglis (2001) remarked that male divers tended to cause more damage on corals than female divers. Again, whether it is gender or education levels, there is a lack of evidence that they are influencing divers" underwater behaviour in a universal way.

Arguably, the environmental beliefs and attitude of the person are aspects that most directly affect a person"s behaviour (Ajzen & Fishbein, 2000; Fishbein & Ajzen, 1975) and divers should be no exception to this. Although this argument is intuitively appealing, results from attitudinal studies are that the relation between attitude and behaviour is inconclusive (Cottrell, 2003). However, Cottrell"s conclusion has not prevented scholars (Musa, Seng, Thirumoorthi & Abessi, 2011; Kler & Tribe, 2012; Moskwa, 2012; Lucrezi et al., 2013) from investigating the psychological and behavioural dimensions (such as motivations, preferences, perceptions, personality and knowledge) of scuba divers.

To systematically understand factors influencing such subjective dimensions, Hungerford & Volk (1990) made a distinction between three types of variables that may influence behaviour. Entry-level variables (ELs) are good predictors of responsible environmental behaviour and may even serve as pre-requisites to other variables in the model. Ownership variables (OVs) are those that are so personal to the individual that one seems to own the issue.

Examples include verbal commitments to the issue, e.g., marine conservation and personally adopted values. Empowerment variables (EVs) are crucial factors in the training of responsible citizens in the environmental dimension. A relevant example is the availability and/or contents of pre-dive briefing given to divers.

This study aims to use empirical findings from Hong Kong divers to explain divers" contact frequency on the marine biota by variables set out in Hungerford & Volk (1990), including equipment carried (EL), verbal commitment to environmental actions (OV), diving experience (EV) and other socio-demographic attributes of divers.

While this is not the first study explaining diver"s underwater behaviour, a major contribution of this study is that actual field data on the exact frequency of contacts on the marine biota are directly measured and used in analyzing the influence of situational as well as attitudinal explanatory variables. In this study, direct observable data for the dependent variable instead of self-reported diving behaviour or perceived impacts are used (c.f. Musa et al., 2010 and Lucrezi et al., 2013) although self-reported data are easier to obtain. Self-reported data may only reflect what the divers would like to be known rather than what they actually did.

Information on the relative importance of predictors offers useful clues for conservationists and dive trip operators to plan and design appropriate measures (see CONCLUSION) to prevent unnecessary damage to the marine biota as a result of diving tourism.

METHODS

Data collected for this study include data on the underwater behaviour of divers, their environmental attitude, commitment and socio-demographic attributes. A total of 115 sets of valid data were collected in 2010 by the following two methods.

Direct Observation

Direct observation of the behaviour of 115 dives from 80 divers during recreational day diving was the main method employed to understand underwater behaviour of scuba divers. Contrary to previous studies where only parts of the dive were observed (Worachananant et al., 2008; Zakai & Chadwick-Furman, 2002), in this study, underwater direct observation covers the entire dive, including descent, dive swimming and ascent. Voluntary research divers were recruited, briefed of the purpose of the research and were given time to familiarize with the record matrix which was used for underwater behaviour recording.

All behaviour recorded were immediately characterised by the research divers into "intentional" or "unintentional" contacts. Intentional contacts were those that the divers were clearly aware of. An example is when divers put their hands on coral mass to steady themselves. Any other contacts or behaviour other than those clearly intentional are considered unintentional. This includes uncertain cases.

As a result, current findings on contact rate are most likely a conservative estimate of the number of intentional contacts and impacts. When the study was conducted, all commercial dive boats in Hong Kong were owned by four dive companies.

Divers participating in the weekend dive trips of all these four companies were selected for observation and completion of questionnaire. Divers with different levels of diving experience and other characteristics (e.g., gender, carrying or not carrying a camera or video-camera) were selected for observation, subject to the agreement of the dive guides of the four dive companies.

On each research trip, the researcher randomly selected a group of divers on board and approached their dive guides on the day of survey for permission to be observed. In order to make minimal distortion on the behaviour of observed divers, the research divers would only explicitly inform and get the permission of the dive guides for observation.

It was up to the dive guide whether to tell the divers that some of them would be watched at that dive. It was acknowledged that even if the dive guide did not inform the scuba divers that they might be observed, it still could not be ensured that recreational divers would not deliberately behave differently because findings showed they might also be aware of being watched without being told (Chung et al., 2013).

Table 1. Descriptive statistics of variables

Independent variables	Mean	Standard deviation
Ownership variables		
OV1[a]: I am willing to pay part of my income (e.g., sewage charges) to reduce environmental pollution.	2.25	0.74
OV2[a]: I am willing to pay part of my income in exchange for better marine conservation.	2.15	0.76
OV3 [a]: I am willing to sacrifice private time to do voluntary work for marine conservation, e.g., Reef Check, beach cleaning…	1.98	0.75
OV4 [a]: I avoid using shampoo or other liquid cleaning agents on boat to avoid polluting the marine environment	1.33	0.59
OV5 [a]: I am willing to pay more for diving in Hong Kong if I know that the extra money will be used to improve marine ecology in Hong Kong	2.19	0.92
OV6 [a]: I avoid conducing scuba diving/snorkeling when visiting coral areas at shallow water or low tides	2.21	1.01
OV7 [a]: Divers should care about marine ecology of Hong Kong	1.35	0.58
OV8[c]: The importance of the morality of an action as a consideration for me to take stance in the 9 statements [b].	2.03	1.15
OV9 [c]: The importance of the legality of an action as a consideration me to take stance in the 9 statements [b].	3.18	1.34
OV10 [c]: The importance of the well-being of the marine environment in Hong Kong as a consideration for me to take stance in the 9 statements [b].	1.80	1.12
Empowerment variable		
EV1: Total number of logged dives to-date	126.55	442.53
Entry level variable		
EL1: Did the diver bring a camera to the dive? (Y=1, N=0)	0.27	0.45
Dependent variables: (contacts made per dive)		
Y_i	3.7	12.29
Y_u	9.3	18.12
Y_t	13.0	23.90

[a] strongly agreed - 1, agreed - 2, neutral - 3, disagree – 4, strongly disagreed – 5

[b] the 9 statements are "eating shark fin", "releasing captivated marine fauna into the sea", "dolphin watching", "eating marine fauna (seafood) captured from the waters around Hong Kong and the seafood is said to be dwindling in number", "promoting Hong Kong as a seafood paradise to promote tourism", "broadcasting of TV episodes that promote the positive image of eating premium seafood caught from the sea", "seeing horseshoe crab lying on the pavement outside seafood restaurants", "buying corals or other marine life for souvenirs or a private aquarium", and "keeping living marine life in a private aquarium".

[c] a rank from 1 to 5 can be assigned with a value of "1" being the most important consideration and "5" means an irrelevant factor.

Questionnaire-Based Survey

A structured questionnaire in bilingual form (Chinese or English) was designed to collect information on the environmental attitudes, values and other socio-demographic data of the observed divers. All divers that were observed underwater were invited to participate in this self-administered questionnaire survey after they finished their dives. Among others, the questionnaire contained questions on their diving experience, impression of the marine environment in Hong Kong, their attitude towards a number of environmental phenomena and their demographic and socio-economic data. Since only one of the 81 divers invited refused to fill the questionnaire, a high response rate of 98.8% was achieved.

Analytical Methods

Classical linear regression is the main method used to estimate the influence of the explanatory variables on the frequency of contacts made by divers. Three models each built with one of the dependent variables, intended contacts made by diver (Y_i), unintended contacts made by diver (Y_u) and total number of contacts made by diver (Y_t) were tested. Each model is explained by the same set of independent variables (see Table 1). All statistical analyses were conducted with SPSS 18.0 (software, Statistical Product and Service Solutions).

RESULTS

The Profile of Respondents

Table 2 summarizes the socio-economic attributes of the respondents. The sample consisted of a greater proportion of male, mostly aged between 20 and 34, was better educated and had higher monthly household income than an averaged Hong Kong citizen. While the demographic characteristics of the sample were not representative of those of Hong Kong citizens, this was of no surprise. Aiming at surveying boat owners, Cottrell (2003) found that his respondents represented a very unique segment of the population: well-educated, affluent, conservative and being male. Similarly, among the 500 divers surveyed diving in Medes Islands, Spain, there were a dominance of male and middle aged divers, and divers with middle or university level education (Mundet & Ribera, 2001). Thus, it is plausible that the sample reflects the typical socio-demographic attributes of recreational divers and not the general population in Hong Kong.

Dependent Variables

The intentional, unintentional and total contact rates for the 80 divers sampled are reported in the last three rows of Table 1.

Ownership Variables

A total of ten ownership variables (OVs) were covered in the question-naire. They consisted of seven statements on divers" own commitments to marine environmental conservation (measured on the 5 point Likert-scale) and three consideration criteria for taking stance on marine actions (see Table 1). Among the OVs, respondents are generally committed to OVs1-7 but are particularly keen on OVs 4 and 7. Among the three considerations for marine action statements (OVs 8-10), Hong Kong divers tend to put greater importance on the well-being of the marine environment. The legality of an action was given an importance level of only 3.18, meaning that respondents might not value legal standards highly in determining their stance on the nine marine action statements (see note b of Table 1).

Entry-Level and Empowerment Variables

Among all the variables tested, only the variable, whether or not the diver brought a camera with him/her in the dive, is identified as entry-level variable (see Table 1). Gender, education levels and age of the divers may be good candidates but none was found to be significant factors in explaining contacts made with the marine biota. There are two possible empowerment variables for the models. The availability of pre-dive briefing may be used as an empowerment variable because in pre-dive briefings, among others, divers will be reminded by their dive guides of ethical and safety etiquettes. However, all divers sampled attended pre-dive briefing and therefore it cannot be used as an explanatory variable in the study. Thus, there only leaves diving experience, measured by the total number of logged dives done to-date, as a possible empowerment variable.

Regression Models

Regressions were attempted twice for each dependent variable. In the first attempt, a total of 15 variables, including OV1 to OV10, EL1, EV1, education, gender and age were all entered into the model. A problem noted with this model specification is that high variance inflation factors (VIFs) were noted for OV1 and OV2 (3.958 and 4.455 respectively). The VIF values indicated that these two variables were collinear and therefore redundant information was found in the models. Owing to these problems, a second attempt was made by omitting OV1 and OV2. In the second attempt, all variables in the regression had normal VIF values. Other results, such as number of significant explanatory variables and d statistics remained similar or same as before.

Table 2. Profile of respondents
(exchange rate: US\$1 = HK\$7.8, October, 2013)

Gender	
Male	65.8%
Female	34.2%
Age	
<19	1.3%
20-34	54.7%
35-49	29.3%
>50	14.7%
Education	
No education/Pre-primary/Primary	0%
Secondary	20.8%
Matriculated	6.5%
Tertiary	51.9%
Post-graduate	20.8%
Averaged per capita monthly income	
Below HK\$3999	1.3%
\$4000-7999	2.5%
\$8000-14999	12.7%
\$15000-29999	29.1%
\$30000-59999	20.3%
Over \$60000	11.4%
I don't want to answer this question	22.8%

Thus, the 13-variable specification was adopted. Table 3 was the regression results of the second attempt.

Standardized coefficients were shown because this showed the greatest effect on the dependent variable despite the differences in the unitary measurements of the independent variables. Based on the d statistics and at 0.05 level of significance, all models fell into the zone of indecision, ie., there was inconclusive evidence of positive autocorrelation (Gujarati, 1998). Only one independent variable (OV4) was found to be significant predictor of the frequencies of all three types of contacts (Y_i, Y_u and Y_t). Bringing a camera to the dive (EL_1) was a significant explanatory variable for intended contact frequency and total contact frequency but not unintended contact frequency.

Table 3. Regression results (n=115)

Dependent variable	Y_i (Model 1)	Y_u (Model 2)	Y_t (Model 3)
	Standardized coefficients[c]		
OV3	-0.063	-0.091	-0.101
OV4	0.309[*]	0.372[*]	0.442[*]
OV5	-0.225[*]	0.010	-0.108
OV6	0.115	-0.108	-0.023
OV7	-0.084	0.172 (p=0.061)	0.087
OV8	-0.045	0.175 (p=0.068)	0.110
OV9	-0.258[*]	-0.114	-0.220[*]
OV10	-0.217[*]	0.035	-0.085
EV1	-0.108	0.094	0.016
EL1	0.351[*]	0.108	0.263[*]
Age[a]	-0.031	-0.053	-0.056
Gender (0=female, 1=male)	0.023	-0.082	-0.051
Education[b]	-0.015	-0.143	-0.116
Model summary Constant	15.262	7.314	22.654
R^2	0.217	0.243	0.272
F	2.158	2.496	2.909
Model significance	0.017	0.005	0.001
Durbin-Watson d statistics	1.524	1.876	1.968

[a] – the actual age as reported by the respondents is used in the model.
[b] –1=no education, 2=primary, 3=secondary, 4=matriculated, 5=tertiary, 6=post-graduate
[c] –effects significant at 0.05 levels are flagged; p value is put in bracket if close to significant.

There are five significant variables in Model 1, meaning that the frequency of intended contacts made with the marine substratum was related to i) whether or not the diver had carried a camera (EL1), ii) diver's perception on the importance of the well-being of the marine environment in Hong Kong (OV10), iii) using the legality of the action as a value judgement criterion (OV9), iv) diver's willingness to pay more to dive for marine conservation purposes (OV5) and v) avoid using polluting shampoos on-board (OV4).

Out of these five variables, two have wrong signs (OV5 & OV10). OV3 also had a wrong sign although it was not a significant explanatory variable. For Model 2, there was just one significant variable (OV4) although two were significant at 10% level (OVs7 & 8). For Model 3, other than OV4, there were two more significant explanatory variables, (OV9 & EL1). All mentioned variables in Models 2 and 3 had the correct signs with respect to the dependent variables.

DISCUSSION

Divers' Behaviour and their Socio-Demographic Attributes

Socio-demographic characteristics of the divers and the empowerment variable (EV1) were not found to be important in predicting their contact frequencies with the marine biota in all cases. While age was not correlated with contact rates in this study, others found that irresponsible underwater behaviour was more frequent among younger divers (Musa et al., 2010). However, as mentioned before, Musa et al. (2010) drew their conclusion from self-reported behavioural intention only.

The coefficients of EV1 were positive for Models 2 and 3 indicating that more experienced divers might actually make more unintentional contacts with the marine biota although this trend was not widespread enough to make EV1 significant. While this appeared counter-intuitive, similar phenomenon was observed by di Franco et al. (2009) who found that divers with higher certification level were making the highest rate of contact in caves. di Franco et al. (2009) surmised that being more confident than others in marine caves was the reason for making more contacts. However, no measurement of confidence was included in this study. The relations between self-confidence and underwater behaviour should be included in similar studies in the future.

Ownership Variables

Several types of OVs are included. Non-economic OVs include OV3, OV4 and OV6. On the other hand, OV5 is an economic OV and OV7 to OV10 are (environmental) value OVs.

Economic and Non-Economic OVs

Among these OVs, the self-reported behaviour of avoid using non-biodegradable shampoos or cleaning agents on board (OV4) was most important in explaining divers" contact rates on marine biota. The significance level of the ordinary least square estimator ranged from 0.000 – 0.003, indicating that the chances that these coefficients were zero in reality was very low. Based on the unstandardized coefficients, for each level of decrease in their agreement with statement (ie., avoid using non-biodegradable shampoos), total contacts with the marine biota in a dive would be increased by about 18 with about 11.5 being unintentional contacts and 6.5 intentional contacts. While there is no obvious reason why the avoidance of non-biodegradable shampoo and not other potentially more relevant environmental attitudinal variables was such a good predictor of a diver"s underwater behaviour, a plausible explanation might be offered. The degree of personal sacrifice called for by OV4 is short-lived and non-economic in nature. Also, the physical setting helps. One dive shop in Hong Kong provides biodegradable liquid cleaners on board free of charge and one of the largest dive boats operating in Hong Kong has no enclosed shower booth on board. On the other hand, while OV6 (i.e, avoid diving or snorkeling in shallow waters or low tide) is similarly a non-economic ownership variable, it is more difficult to be put into practice because most of the popular dive sites in Hong Kong are quite shallow (<10 m) and where to dive is often determined by the dive guide and not the divers themselves. Thus, it may be argued that it is more possible for divers to agree to OV4 than OV6. In order to test how valid this explanation is, future research should collect information on other non-economic OVs that only require short-term personal sacrifice.

Environmental Value OVs

Other than OV4, the coefficients of three other OVs were found to significantly different from zero in Model 1. All of them were negatively affecting rates of intentional contacts. Regression results showed that a one-point increase in OV10 (ie., valuing the well-being of marine environment in Hong Kong less in taking environmental stance) will lead to a reduction of 2.4

intended contacts per dive. The same reduction in intended contact (2.4) can also be explained by a one-point increase in OV9 (ie., valuing the legality of the action less in taking environmental stance). The former is counter-intuitive because it is generally believed that environmentally friendly actions, ie., reduced contact with marine biota are grounded on environmental values. The latter is not as counter-intuitive as the former because the legality of an action may not be consistent with its environmental desirability. The coefficient of OV8 also has a wrong sign although it is not statistically significant. The conclusion so far is that the disciplined action of sampled divers seems to ground on neither legal consideration nor ethical attitude nor considerations of the well-being of the marine environment.

The unstandardized coefficient of OV5 is -3.073 meaning that for each level of increase in the unwillingness to pay more for diving, there is a reduction in 3 intentional contacts per dive even though the extra money paid will be used to improve marine ecology. This relation between OV5 and Y_i is counter-intuitive, only if it is assumed that divers who care not to make intended contacts with the marine biota (i.e., willing to discipline own behaviour) are equally willing to financially contribute to marine ecology improvement. This assumption however lacks empirical support. Thus, it may be concluded that environmentally well-behaved divers in the sample are not as willing to pay for improvement in marine ecology as the less well-behaved divers.

Not surprisingly, Y_u is the hardest to be explained by attitudinal factors and it is also not related to the use of camera underwater. The coefficient of two OVs are found to be significant if an α error of 7% is tolerated. A one-point increase in OV7 (i.e., a decrease in agreement with the statement that divers/snorkelers should care about marine ecology of Hong Kong) and OV8 (i.e., valuing the morality of an action less in taking environmental stance) will increase unintended contacts by 5.6 and 2.8 per dive respectively. The independent variables have the right signs.

Recall that the environmental value OVs have wrong signs in Model 1. Thus, it may be concluded that environmental value OVs are better explanatory variables for unintended contacts than intended contacts.

Entry Level Variables

Doing underwater photography is considered an EL. The coefficients are significantly different from zero for both Models 1 and 3. A camera-carrying diver will increase intended contact with the marine biota by 9.8 and total contact by 14.2 per dive. During underwater photography, divers often need to steady themselves in water to get the image focused. This explains why photo-taking divers make more intended contacts than their non-camera carrying counterparts. Our findings are consistent with those of Barker (2003) and Worachananant et al. (2008). Barker (2003) found that being a photographer increased contact rate by 0.211 per minute of dive. With an average dive time of about 25 minutes for this study, it will mean about 5 contacts per dive for being a photographer. Although this contact rate for being a photographer is just about half of that found in this study, it is consistent with the main trend that samples in this study tend to make higher rate of contacts (Chung et al., 2013) with the marine biota than those studied by Barker (2003). Although Rouphael & Inglis (2001) also found that camera used by relatively "naïve divers" would not necessarily increase damage to the reef, this should not be considered a contradiction of this study since our samples should belong to the more specialised underwater photographer category (as opposed to the "naïve divers") in Rouphael & Inglis's study (2001) who were also found to cause most damages to the reef.

The Best Fit Model

While all the three models are significant, not many significant explanatory variables are identified. Also, for all models, only slightly more than 20% and up to 27% of the total variation in the Ys can be explained by the regression models. Thus, it is concluded that divers" rate of contact with the marine biota is only marginally related to ownership and empowerment variables. Yet, it should be mentioned that statistical models using personal values, attitudes and socio-demographic data to explain environmental behaviour generally suffers from relatively low explanatory power. For instance, in the six models constructed by Ramkissoon, Smith & Weiler (2013) to explain the intention for pro-environmental behaviour with various attitudinal and value variables, the explanatory power ranged from the high of 30% to a low of 10%.

Limitations of the Study

Barker (2003) and di Franco et al. (2009) found that divers" contact rates vary significantly with the topography of dive sites. Cave and plateau were noted to associate with higher contact rates. However, dive site topography was not included in this study because there was a lack of variations in the topography of popular dive sites in Hong Kong. All popular dive sites are sloping reef-based sites; and there are also no cave, wall or fringing reef sites in Hong Kong. Another deficiency is that no measurement of self-confidence of divers is included. Thus, the author is not able to validate if the higher rate of intended contacts of experienced divers is a result of their greater self-confidence.

Another limitation of this study is the small sample size. The sample size in this study is the smallest among two similar studies, namely Barker (2003) and di Franco et al. (2009). Barker (2003) studied the underwater behaviour of 353 divers and di Franco et al. (2009) collected the self-reported behaviour of 302 divers. However, this study also has merits over these two studies. The author collected data on actual contact rate and the one-to-one ratio (ie., one research diver only need to observe one recreational diver) used in making underwater observation in this study also mean that it was less likely to miss any remarkable behaviour (including contacts with reef) of the divers in this study. Since Barker (2003) did not include attitudinal variables in her study, this study remained the only such study that the author was aware of to connect attitudinal variables with actual observable behaviour for divers.

CONCLUSION

Many studies have shown that scuba diving generally would cause some degree of damage to the marine biota. Yet, our knowledge about why scuba divers may damage the marine environment is incomplete. This chapter fills the lacuna of current literature by identifying the empowerment, ownership and other diver specific variables that can explain the observed underwater behaviour of divers.

Consistent with previous studies, camera-carrying divers made more contacts with the marine biota. A camera-carrying diver will increase intended contact with the marine biota by 9.8 and total contact by 14.2 per dive. While it is generally believed that giving precautionary warning in the pre-dive briefing may help reduce such impact, Rouphael & Inglis (2001) also pointed out that verbal warning might have little effect on especially the goal-directed specialised underwater photographers.

Socio-demographic characteristics of the divers and diving experience (EV) are not found to be important in predicting divers" contact frequencies with the marine biota. Among the varieties of OVs tested, non-economic OV that demanded short-lived personal sacrifice (avoid using non-biodegradable shampoo) was found to be an important criterion in distinguishing a low contact diver from a normal diver. Results also showed that even more disciplined divers were not so willing to pay more for marine conservation and their disciplined behaviour was grounded on neither the legal consideration, nor ethical attitude, nor considerations of the well-being of the marine environment.

Unintended contacts however was the hardest to explain probably because they were influenced by many external confounding factors which were hard to capture or quantify for statistical analysis. This limitation is reflected in the overall explanatory power of the models that only slightly more than 20% and up to 27% of the total variation in the contact rates can be explained by the regression models. As a result, there appears to be some other stronger but unknown factors at work to influence the underwater behaviour of divers. While it is commonly thought that education can be used to reduce the impact on the marine biota from scuba diving, it is likely that such a soft approach may not be effective in minimizing the damage from scuba diving on the reef. A more effective measure to reduce divers" intended contacts with the marine biota, including those from avid underwater photographer is to introduce dive guide intervention on the spot. Yet, such third party intervention is less effective in reducing unintended contacts which are more strongly influenced by specific physical and contextual factors. In all, a multi-pronged approach is required to more effectively reduce both intended and unintended damage on the reef by scuba divers.

REFERENCES

Ajzen, I., & Fishbein, M. (2000). The prediction of behaviour from attitudinal and normative variables. In E. Tory, & A.W. Kruglanski (Eds.), Motivational science: social & personality perspectives (pp.177-190). Philadelphia, USA: Psychology Press.

Barker, N.H.L. (2003). Ecological and socio-economic impacts of dive and snorkel tourism in St. Lucia, West Indies [Unpublished doctoral thesis]. University of York, York.

Chen, X.D., Peterson, M.N., Hull, V., Lu, C.T., Lee, G.D., Hong, D.Y., & Liu, J.G. (2011). Effects of attitudinal and sociodemographic factors on pro-environmental behaviour in urban China. *Environmental Conservation*, 38, 45-52.

Chung, S.S., Au, C.S., & Qiu, J.W. (2013). Understanding and managing the underwater behaviour of scuba divers. *Environmental Management*, 51, 824-837.

Cottrell, S.P. (2003). Influence of scoiodemographics and environmental attitudes on general responsible environmental behaviour among recreational boaters. *Environment and Behaviour*, 35, 347-375.

di Franco, A., Milazzo, M., Baiata, P., Tomasello, A. & Chemello, R. (2009). Scuba diver behaviour and its effects on the biota of a Mediterranean marine protected area. *Environmental Conservation*, 36, 32-40.

Fishbein, J. & Ajzen, I. (1975). Belief, Attitude, Intention, and Behaviour. Reading, UK: Addison-Wesley.

Guzner, B., Novplansky, A., Shalit, O., & Chadwick, N.E. (2010). Indirect impacts of recreational scuba diving; patterns of growth and predation in branching stony corals. *Bulletin of Marine Science*, 86, 727-742.

Gujarati, D.N. (1998). Essentials of Econometrics (2nd edition). Boston, USA: Irwin McGraw-Hill.

Hawkins, J.P., & Roberts, C.M. (1992). Effects of recreational scuba diving on fore-reef slope communities of coral reefs. *Biological Conservation*, 62, 171-178.

Hawkins, J., Roberts, C.M., van't Hof, T., de Meyer, K., Tratalos, J., & Aldam, C. (1999). Effects of recreational scuba diving on Caribbean coral and fish communities. *Conservation Biology*, 13, 888-897.

Hungerford, H.R., & Volk, T. L. (1990). Changing learner behaviour through environmental education. *Journal of Environmental Education*, 21, 8-21.

Hunter, L.M., Hatch, A., & Johnson, A. (2004). Cross-national gender variation in environmental behaviours. *Social Science Quarterly*, 85, 677-694.

Jones, R.E., & Dunlap, R.E. (1992). The social bases of environmental concern: have they changed over time? *Rural Sociology*, 57, 28–47.

Kler, B.K., & Tribe, J. (2012). Flourishing through scuba: understanding the pursuit of dive experiences. Tourism in Marine Environments, 8, 19-32.

Lucrezi, S., Saayman, M., & van der Merwe, P. (2013). Managing diving impacts on reef ecosystems: analysis of putative influences of motivations, marine life preferences and experience on divers" environmental perceptions. *Ocean and Coastal Management*, 76, 52-63.

Moskwa, E.C. (2012). Exploring place attachment: an underwater perspective. Tourism in Marine Environments, 8, 33-46.

Mundet, L., & Ribera, L. (2001). Characteristics of divers at a Spanish resort. Tourism Management, 22, 501-510.

Musa, G., Seng, W.T., Thirumoorthi, T., & Abessi, M. (2011). The influence of scuba divers" personality, experience, and demographic profile on their underwater behaviour. *Tourism in Marine Environments*, 7, 1-14.

Ramkissoon, H., Smith, L.D.G., & Weiler, B. (2013). Relationships between place attachment, place satisfaction and pro-environmental behaviour in an Australian national park. *Journal of Sustainable Tourism*, 21, 434-457.

Rouphael, A.B., & Inglis, G.J. (2001). "Take only photographs and leave only footprint"?: An experimental study of the impacts of underwater photographers on coral reef dive sites. *Biological Conservation*, 100, 281-287.

Scott, D., & Willits, F.K. (1994). Environmental attitudes and behaviour: a Pennsylvania survey. *Environment and Behaviour*, 26, 239-260.

Smith, K., Scarr, M. & Scarpaci, C. (2010). Grey nurse shark (*Carcharias Taurus*) diving tourism: tourist compliance and shark behaviour at Fish Rock, Australia. *Environmental Management*, 46, 699-710.

Stern, P.C., Dietz, T., & Kalof, L. (1993). Value orientations, gender, and environmental concern. *Environment and Behaviour*, 25, 322-348.

Thapa, B., Graefe, A.R., & Meyer, L.A. (2006). Specialization and marine based environmental behaviours among SCUBA divers. *Journal of Leisure Research*, 38, 601-615.

Walters, R.D.M., & Samways, M.J. (2001). Sustainable dive ecotourism on a South African coral reef. Biodiversity and Conservation, 10, 2167-2179.

Woodland, D.J., & Hooper, J.N.A. (1977) The effect of human trampling on coral reefs. *Biological Conservation*, 11, 1-4.

Worachananant, S., Carter, R.W., Hockings, M., & Reopanichkul, P. (2008). Managing the impacts of SCUBA divers on Thailand"s coral reefs. *Journal of Sustainable Tourism*, 16, 645-663.

Zakai, D., & Chadwick-Furman, N.E. (2002). Impacts of intensive recreational diving on reef corals at Eilat, northern Red Sea. *Biological Conservation*, 105, 179-187.

In: Ecotourism   ISBN: 978-1-63482-027-1
Editor: Shannon C. Brophy   © 2015 Nova Science Publishers, Inc.

Chapter 6

EVALUATING SUSTAINABLE TOURISM USING INDICATORS: PROBLEMS AND SOLUTIONS

Georges A. Tanguay* and Juste Rajaonson†

Tourism and Heritage Research Center, School of Management,
University of Quebec in Montreal, Canada

ABSTRACT

This chapter focuses on the selection and use of sustainability indicators in the field of tourism. First, we begin by drawing up the context that makes the use of indicators an important approach in the management of sustainable tourism. Second, we address three main issues related to the use of sustainability indicators in tourism studies: i) the trade-off between the scientific and political approaches; ii) the potential role of indicators in tourism development policy planning, and iii) the interpretation of the indicators" score following their calculation. Finally, we discuss the implications of these proposals on research and public policy.

* E-mail: tanguay.georges@uqam.ca.
† E-mail: rajaonson.juste@courrier.uqam.ca.

1. INTRODUCTION

Sustainable tourism development has become a major objective for tourist destinations. Its adoption is reflected in the implementation of various measures to improve their economic, socio-cultural and environmental performance (Ahn et al., 2002; Castellani & Sala, 2010). These measures grouped under the banner of sustainable tourism take many forms, including: i) the coordination of public interventions, policy, regulation, and management to preserve and promote local and regional tourism products; ii) economic incentives to make practices more sustainable and equitable, and iii) measures to educate visitors on the socioeconomic and environmental issues in tourism. Their implementation led to multiple benefits for many destinations over the world. First, tourism became more profitable to the economy of many destinations worldwide (Manning & Dougherty, 1995; Wahab & Pigram, 2010). Second, it also became less damaging to their cultural, urban and natural heritage (Stabler, 2007; Mowforth & Munt, 2008). Finally, in specific cases, tourism played an important role in the revitalization of both rural and urban communities (Hunter, 1997; World Tourism Organization, 2004).

Because of the positive impact of these measures illustrated in best practice inventories, such as in Weaver (2006) and Stabler (2007), several tourist destinations started to apply sustainable tourism principles. They invested in various projects in this regard and must be accountable to taxpayers and national government. Thus: i) measuring the benefits of these investments; ii) reporting on the impacts of projects on the environment, society and economy, and iii) complying with legislative and policy frameworks of national governments, are among the reasons that led to the use of sustainability indicators as central instruments for tourist destinations (Roberts & Tribes, 2008). Additionally, their use allows for more transparent assessment and monitoring of tourism sustainability (Ko, 2005; Choi & Sirakaya, 2006; Castellani & Sala, 2010). Indicators were also described and recognized as measurement tools, which can be adapted to each destination to fit its context (Miller, 2001). This flexibility, however, has not been helpful to better guide the assessment of sustainable tourism. Rather, it contributed to the proliferation of case studies featuring customized approach and indicators to each destination (Tanguay et al., 2013). This trend justified by the specificity of each destination and context amplified the lack of consensus about the concept of sustainable tourism. Thus, this diversity of approaches fuelled criticism of the concept of sustainable tourism, deeming it inconsistent and easy to manipulate for political advantage. However, a review of these approaches allows for identification of common indicators whose relevance is generally recognized in the literature (Tanguay et al., 2013).

Today, the use of indicators is an important part of sustainable tourism planning. It is generally preferred over other existing approaches such as ecological footprint and life cycle assessment for four main reasons. First, it has the ability to easily capture the multiple dimensions of sustainable tourism compared to the other approaches, which often reduce the analysis to a single dimension (e.g., monetization). Second, the indicators are relatively easy to interpret (e.g., energy consumption), compared to other tools, which typically involve the creation of a new scale of values (e.g., ecological footprint). Third, other approaches such as life cycle assessment require more complex calculation steps and modelling, which make them difficult instruments to be used in contemporary decision-making processes involving stakeholders with different levels of expertise. Finally, indicator assessment is relatively flexible and can be adjusted according to the objectives of the evaluation approach, (e.g., backcasting vs. forecasting), their users and recipients, (e.g., experts vs. citizens), and the type of information, (e.g., quantitative vs. qualitative). Nonetheless, Gasparatos et al. (2012), specify the main weakness of this approach: its dependence on methodological choices such as weighting. According to Ness et al. (2007), the methodological dependence is inherent in any process of analysis in the social sciences and simply requires greater scientific transparency. Additionally, prior to their use, indicators must be selected. As addressed in the next section, the selection of indicators raises a critical issue regarding the necessary trade-off between scientific and political approaches to sustainability indicators.

2. SELECTION OF INDICATORS: BRIDGING ACADEMIC AND POLICYMAKER PERSPECTIVES

The selection of indicators often raises a debate opposing two perspectives. The first one is scientific-oriented. From this perspective, sustainable tourism is viewed as a complex object requiring the use of sophisticated techniques and equally complex scientific methods to measure and monitor (Rajaonson & Tanguay, 2012). Hence, the indicators are often developed and described using technical terms relevant to experts (Schianetz & Kavanagh, 2008). This would explain why these indicators often fail to gain legitimacy among policymakers and civil society, despite their relevance. The second perspective is policy-oriented. It is based on the needs and policy objectives to justify the development of indicators (Bouni, 1998; Reed et al., 2006). The resulting set of indicators is often the result of a consensus among the stakeholders rather than a neutral and reproducible system. It introduces subjectivity, given that the content and priorities raised by the indicators depend on the interests of the stakeholders involved in the process. Given these findings, an approach where the choice of indicators reflects both scientific and political perspectives is desirable and will contribute to the scientific legitimacy of indicators, while ensuring their relevance for policymakers (Rametsteiner et al., 2010; Tanguay & Rajaonson, 2012).

To address the integration of these two perspectives, Tanguay et al. (2013) proposed a strategy, which was used to develop a set of sustainable tourism indicators for the region of Gaspésie-Îles-de-la-Madeleine in Quebec (Rajaonson & Tanguay, 2012). The strategy's objective was threefold: i) to address the scientific concerns by developing indicators that take into account what the literature proposes as the most pertinent indicators while ensuring coverage of all the dimensions of sustainability; ii) to address the policymakers" concerns by ensuring their consistency with the destination's policy framework, and iii) to prevent conflicts of interest that would result from an approach essentially based on local actors" decisions by using common indicators that will ultimately allow for comparison with other destinations.

The strategy begins with an extensive inventory of potential indicators based on the ones propose in the World Tourism Organization's *Indicators of Sustainable Development for Tourism Destinations: A Guidebook* (World Tourism Organization, 2004). This initial inventory comprises 768 indicators developed by a wide range of academics and experts. After dropping several indicators because of redundancy and irrelevance to the context of the Canadian regions, this extensive list dropped to 506 indicators. Two sets of selection criteria were successively applied to these 506 indicators in order to reduce this list to an optimal number.

Then, a primary set of four criteria was developed to reduce this list of 506 indicators. It includes: i) the classification of the indicators into the dimensions and sub-dimensions of sustainable tourism; ii) the frequency of use of the indicators, in order to ensure that the selected indicators are of generally recognized pertinence and value; ii) the ability to reproduce the coverage of the main sustainable tourism dimensions of the initial indicators, which serves as the selection threshold for the most frequently used indicators, and iii) the measurability overtime, allowing for follow up of improvement and progress.

Next, a secondary set of three criteria was applied to this selection, which allows for adjustment of the indicators to the specific policy context of the destination. This ensures: i) the availability of data, and in certain cases the replacement of some indicators to maintain the coverage of issues of sustainable tourism; ii) the compatibility of the indicators with the policy of the destinations through matching the indicators to the policy framework of the destinations, and iii) the validation of the indicators with the stakeholders to confirm their comprehension and usefulness. The entire process is illustrated in Figure 1 and allows for the identification of 20 indicators of sustainable tourism, which can support the policy framework for the two Quebec tourism regions" case study. The indicators are shown in Table 1.

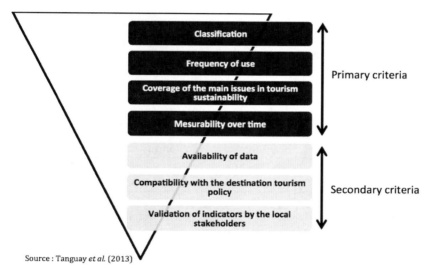

Source : Tanguay *et al.* (2013)

Figure 1. Selection Criteria of Key Sustainable Tourism Indicators.

The indicators" selection strategy was successfully applied to two Quebec tourism regions. Two key lessons can be learned. First, it allows for identifying gaps in current statistics on sustainable tourism in Quebec, which call for various levels of government to improve the data collection as well as the available information required for such an evaluation. This problem is not specific to Quebec, but is prevalent in other areas as well (Rajaonson & Tanguay, 2012). Second, it provides an example of how scientific expertise and local experience can be better integrated (Tanguay et al., 2013). On one hand, the development of guidelines for the regions" tourism policy involved the main local and regional stakeholders. On the other, external expertise was entrusted with the development of indicators for monitoring and evaluation of the objectives of the resulted policy guidelines. This helped select relevant indicators, which ensure proper coverage of the main dimensions of sustainable tourism and prevent from the adoption of too specific assessment indicators. Such a strategy is also applicable to other destinations due to its flexibility, and have the ability to ensure the validity and credibility of the indicators used to assess the achievement of sustainable tourism. As we show in the next section, following their selection and assessment, indicators can play important roles in the decision-making process.

Table 1. The 20 STI Satisfying the Four General Selection Criteria

Issues	Indicators
Ecosystem	Protect natural area
Water	Water consumption (tourism sector)
Atmosphere	Air pollution (tourism sector)
Energy	Energy consumption (tourism sector)
Waste	Volume of recycled or treated waste/total volume generated
Well-being	Level of satisfaction of the local population
Resilience and risk	Environmental vulnerability
Security and safety	Ratio of tourists to local population at cultural events
Health	Quality of bodies of water (lakes, rivers, sea)
Satisfaction	Level of tourist satisfaction
Public participation	Level of public participation in election
Culture	Level of maintenance of heritage sites
Accessibility	Use of transport modes to the destination
Investments	% of new tourism real estate developments
Promotion of ecotourism	Number of businesses labelled eco-responsible
Economic vitality	% of income generated by tourism in the community
Employment	% of new jobs in the tourism sector occupied by local residents
Marketing	% of return visits
Distinction	Number of visits to heritage and cultural sites
Tourist traffic	Volume of tourists

Source: Tanguay et al. (2013).

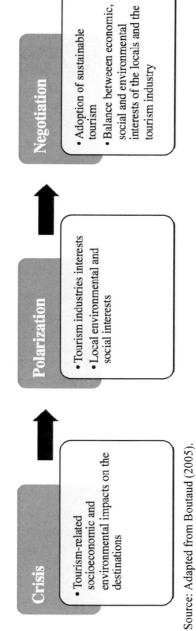

Source: Adapted from Boutaud (2005).

Figure 2. Sustainable Tourism from a Negotiation Perspective.

3. ROLES OF INDICATORS IN TOURISM DEVELOPMENT POLICY PLANNING

Indicators often play a retrospective role that consists of identifying the aspects in which the destinations were successful and the other aspects where they needed to make progress (Gahin et al., 2003). It also aims to estimate the magnitude of these findings and to identify the most influential endogenous factors (Choi & Sirakaya, 2006). The existence of accreditations, labels, and performance benchmarking for sustainable tourism destinations, show the importance of this retrospective role in the literature and practice (World Tourism Organization, 2004; Weaver, 2006; Stabler, 2007; Castellani & Sala, 2010).

Nevertheless, indicators may also play a prospective role when they are used as assessment criteria, for example, in the decision-making process leading to the selection and prioritization of projects. This prospective role of indicators as inputs to decision-making or as project or policy implementation criteria is still underdeveloped in the literature. It involves the interpretation of the indicators based on the achievement of established performance objectives (Tanguay & Rajaonson, 2013). This prospective role requires further methodological specifications related to aggregation and weighting, which often limit its study in the literature. Thus, the aggregation of indicators into indices is not something that researchers and experts always agree upon. Critics of this method prefer to avoid the aggregation of indicators to keep as much information in the interpretation of observations as possible for the purpose of planning (Saisana & Tarantola, 2002). However, supporters emphasize the importance of aggregation in order to render indicators simpler and more comprehensive for decision-making processes where multiple stakeholders with divergent interests are involved (Wong, 2006). There are several approaches to aggregating indicators. For example, the classification of indicators from statistical methods is increasingly used to avoid ambiguity in specifying dimensions that are often overlapping (Blancas et al., 2011). To be reliable, however, these methods require a large amount of comprehensive and comparable data from multiple destinations. As an alternative, destinations may refer to the policy objectives they identified through a participatory process. Although the indicators may adequately cover the identified objectives, they are at risk of omitting other relevant issues of sustainable tourism. Therefore, the use of the three main dimensions of sustainable development (i.e., economic, socio-cultural and environmental) as the organizational framework of indicators remains relevant at this point. The triple bottom-line is often preconized since it has brought researchers, experts, policymakers and other stakeholders to a consensus, despite differences and numerous attempts at re-conceptualization.

Complementarily, once indices are created, it becomes possible to establish the relative importance of dimensions by applying weighting rules. This step is relevant in a decision-making process when choosing and planning future projects based on multiple criteria or when there are many objectives to achieve. One of the most intuitive rules to establish a weighting system is based on a qualitative assessment of a group of experts. The resulting weighting system allows for the broadest consensus. However, a convergence of opinions is not always possible, particularly for complex issues such as sustainable development or tourism. Therefore, the use of mathematical rules to develop the weighting system can be considered. For example, Blancas et al. (2011) uses the distance to the "anti-target" to measure and compare sustainable tourism in Portuguese tourist destinations. In this case, the reference value of each indicator is the minimum value observed in the assessed destinations. Accordingly, a greater coefficient is attributable to the indicators, which show a value that is farther to the reference value. Another approach that is consistent with the Blancas et al. (2011) approach consists of a relative assessment of indicators against a year of reference or against the attainment of a future goal. In the first case, we seek to give greater weight to indicators where a weak value is observed, because it is towards the aspects related to these indicators that the action plan and future projects would be developed. In the second case, the emphasis is on achieving the objectives. In the latter case, projects that are proposed in the future are evaluated based on their contribution to achieving the target values of the indicators and indices. The more the project helps to advance the goals, the more it will be favoured.

To illustrate this role of indicators and its contribution to decision-making process, Tanguay & Rajaonson (2013) investigate how the assessment of sustainable tourism indicators of a destination can be used to define targets and thus select among different projects the ones that allow for reducing the gap to the target, taking into account various constraints. Two main lessons can be learned.

First, the analysis illustrates how indicators can be used in decision-making process based on the assessment of different projects (e.g., historic building maintenance; new building development; public space expansion) and the selection of the one that allows for achieving the policy objectives previously established. Such assessment is likely to complement existing approaches, such as cost-benefit and multi-criteria analysis. Thus, it allows for identifying the project whose implementation helps arrive at the best policy objectives reflected by the sustainability indicators. For this purpose, the indicators are converted into projects or policy achievement tools. This implies that once quantified, the indicators undergo a series of operations. For example, the distance to a target value can be used to choose among different projects that help achieving the goal previously set or at least allow moving towards better performance (e.g., higher direct revenues from tourism; lower negative water quality impact; safer area for locals). This selection process implies that the destination has established a series of goals reflected by the indicators that are quantifiable, realistic and ambitious enough and that the planned projects are designed to approximate these goals. Furthermore, the aggregation of the indicators must ensure that higher values in environmental indicators don't compensate for lower values in socioeconomic indicators and vice-versa.

Second, the comparison of the expected impacts of different projects on indicators and indices of sustainable tourism is just one example to illustrate how the knowledge and information provided by the sustainability indicators can be enriched and further implemented in planning for future tourism policies. In fact, there are other aspects of the integration of sustainability principles into decision-making processes that call for further research. For example, the development of stronger links between the indicators, the target values and project selection for future policies is still overlooked. As Blanca et al. (2011) argue, the development of such tools will enable to acquire more transparent yet precise information from the use of sustainability indicators in tourism policy development than just a descriptive statistics on the destination performance. Finally, there is also another aspect of sustainability assessment that is overlooked in the literature, which is addressed in the next section: the interpretation of the indicators following their calculation.

4. INTERPRETATION OF THE INDICATORS FOLLOWING THEIR CALCULATION

The most successful destinations for sustainable tourism are usually designated on the basis of their scores for a range of given economic, socio-cultural and environmental indicators. This interpretation of indicators is relatively limited and has two main weaknesses. It underestimates the problems of possible counterbalancing between indicator values, particularly when they are aggregated. Thus, a destination could show an overall positive assessment with a relatively high score for a given indicator despite a negative score for other indicators. Interpretation may not be accurate even using computational methods such as *Borda rule* that is designed to minimize potential counterbalancing between indicator values. This is due to considerable variation in scores from one indicator to another and from one destination to another. In addition, an interpretation based solely on the indicators" value minimizes the inherent temporal dimension to the concept of sustainable tourism (Bell & Morse, 2008). Indeed, it does not take into account the progress made by cities, for example, in relation to a reference year. A destination could show a relatively greater result and yet have declined relative to a reference year. Because of these problems, interpretation of indicators based solely on their score is insufficient to determine the most sustainable destinations and requires a greater reflection on the evaluation criteria of sustainable tourism indicators.

In light of these observations, we propose three criteria for evaluation of sustainable tourism to allow for a more detailed interpretation of the indicators used: i) a high score on these indicators; ii) a minimum of compensation between socioeconomic and environmental indicators, and iii) improved scores over time. We explain below their relevance based on their ability to capture the three concepts inherent in the concept of sustainable tourism, namely: the multidimensionality, the search for a compromise between the anthropocentric and environmentalist visions of sustainable tourism, and the notion of progress over time.

Criterion 1: A High Value of the Indicators

The first criterion is generally used to interpret sustainability indicators in the existing literature. It consists of identifying the most successful destinations in terms of sustainability on the basis of the score of the indicators measured. The relevance of this criterion is closely related to the use of indicators in the analysis of sustainable tourism. It is based on the ability of indicators to capture the multidimensionality of sustainable tourism by expressing it as a simple and accessible economic, social and environmental performance value (Macarena et al., 2012). Thus, the relevance of this criterion is primarily attributed to its methodological value for scientists. Indeed, the use of indicators to operationalize the concept of sustainable tourism by translating it into observable and measurable variables can allow for empirical verification. It then allows for using quantitative and qualitative analysis tools to further describe sustainability characteristics of the destinations or explain phenomena such as tourist attractiveness and destination competitiveness. Finally, the relevance of this criterion is assigned to its normative value for policymakers to the extent that it measures progress or the attainment of a number of objectives defined in the context of tourism development policies (Castellani & Sala, 2010).

Criterion 2: Addressing Counterbalance Issues among Economic, Social and Environmental Indicators

When interpreting the indicators" value, high scores for a given indicators can compensate for other indicators with relatively lower scores. In such a case, the interpretation of scores can be problematic. For example, a destination can be classified in the lead due to an exceptional score for a particular dimension. To address this problem, we propose to complete interpretation of the indicators by applying a second criterion, which takes into account a minimum achievement level of economic, social and environmental performance and which aims to assess cities based on the level of trade-off among economic, social and environmental performance. Thus, the most successful cities are those with a high score in all the three dimensions. This will overcome the problem of counterbalancing. The relevance of this criterion is justified by its ability to reflect the desired compromise between two visions of sustainable tourism. One is centered on the interests of tourists and the tourism industry and the other is centered on the local population and environment. Accordingly, this criterion allows taking into account the constant negotiation between these two interests in achieving sustainability in tourism, which comprises three steps. First, the negotiation is usually initiated by a crisis. In the case of sustainable tourism, it is the awareness of the socioeconomic and environmental issues attributed to the growth of tourism activities in tourist destinations. Second, the negotiation involves a conflict that promotes polarization of interests. In the case of sustainable tourism, this polarization is caused by two fundamental ideological positions: a) the supporters of a focus on sustainable tourism that will lead to higher revenue which, in turn, will improve quality of life of the locals and allow for better infrastructure and means to preserve heritage and environment and b) the advocates of the primacy of social and environmental interests of the locals who believe tourism will cause environmental degradation and depletion of resources, but which, in the long run, will limit the capacity of territories to meet current and future tourism activities. Finally, the negotiation leads to the search for a compromise, and the demand for an optimal solution. In the case of sustainable tourism, this optimal solution refers to the recognition of the equal importance of the above interests and the adoption of policies aimed at finding a balance between these two concerns. This is illustrated in Figure 2.

Criterion 3: Improvement over Time

Achieving sustainability implies being consistent with improvements in the economic, social and environmental aspects over time. An increase in performance over time is desirable because it indicates the extent to which the destination has holistically addressed the positive and negative impacts of tourism on its overall sustainable development. This criterion is particularly relevant in assessing tourism sustainability using indicators because it is the main rationale behind investments in policies and projects that are geared towards sustainability. In fact, the adoption of a sustainable tourism policy generally aims to address three specific issues, including: i) increased demand for tourist goods and services that are less harmful to the environment and cultural heritage; ii) public interventions to address the problems underlying tourism activities in order to attract visitors; iii) public interventions in regard to unbalanced tourism in urban and rural destinations; iv) the conversion of political discourses on sustainability into concrete actions in order to be accountable to taxpayers and tourism operators, and v) compliance with the normative policies of sustainability imposed by higher levels of government. Finally, an analysis of the improvement of the indicators" value overtime provides complementary information about the value of the indicators themselves. It allows for assessing the extent to which investment and projects under the banner of sustainable practices have addressed the issues for which they were developed.

CONCLUSION

The conclusion is threefold. First, from a research perspective, sustainability indicators have been the subject of extensive literature and are likely to mobilize more research in the future. In the field of tourism, the last

25 years of research on sustainability indicators have showcased the strengths and weaknesses of many destinations and have helped in defining the best destinations. However, there are still several aspects of sustainability indicators that can be improved and these issues will continue to mobilize research. Three of these issues were addressed in the present chapter. The first one is the search for a trade-off between science and policy approaches to the selection of sustainability indicators prior to their assessment and use. We argued that such a trade-off could be achieved by a careful selection of indicators in order to ensure the quality of indicators and their relevance to the overall dimensions of sustainable tourism. This would be done in collaboration with local stakeholders to ensure that the indicators are relevant to the policy objectives of the destination.

The second issue we addressed is that of bringing the indicators into the policy implementation and planning process. We argued that it is possible to provide a broader role to the indicators by converting them into criteria for choosing between several projects and policy measures. This will lead to extend the typical retrospective role for the indicators to a prospective role in the decision-making process. This latter will allow for a better link between indicator assessment, policy planning and effective project selection.

Finally, we addressed the issue relative to the interpretation of the indicators following their calculation. We argued that indicators" assessment approach for selecting the most successful destination based on the indicators" value is limited since it does not take into account the important trade-off among economic, social and environmental interests, and the improvements over time, which are important criteria for sustainability. As the contribution of these criteria to the use of sustainability indicators in tourism studies is yet to be empirically investigated, we acknowledge that they have the potential to provide further characteristics of sustainable tourism and will help in identifying the most "sustainable" destination.

REFERENCES

Ahn, B. Y., Lee, B. K. & Shafer, C. S. (2002). Operationalizing Sustainability InRegional Tourism Planning: An Application of the Limits of Acceptable Change Framework. *Tourism Management*, 23 (1), 1-15.

Bell, S. & Morse, S. (2008). *Sustainability Indicators: Measuring the Immeasurable?* London: Earthscan, 2ème édition.

Blancas, F. J., Lozano-Oyola, M., González, M., Guerrero, F. M. & Caballero, R. (2011). How to Use Sustainability Indicators for Tourism Planning: The Case of Rural Tourism in Andalusia (Spain). *Science of the Total Environment*, 412/413, 28-45.

Bouni, C. (1998). L'enjeu des indicateurs de développement durable. Mobiliser des besoins pour concrétiser des principes. *Nature, Sciences et Société*, 6 (3), 18-26.

Boutaud, A. (2005). *Le développement durable: Penser le changement ou changer le pansement?* Lyon: University of Jean Monnet.

Castellani, V. & Sala, S. (2010). Sustainable Performance Index for Tourism Policy Development. *Tourism Management*, 31 (6), 871-880.

Choi, H. C. & Sarakaya, E. (2006). Sustainability Indicators for Managing Community Tourism. *Tourism Management*, 27 (6), 1274-1289.

Hunter, C. (1997). Sustainable Tourism as an Adaptive Paradigm. *Annals of Tourism Research*, 24(4), 850-867.

Ko, T. G. (2005). Development of a Tourism Sustainability Assessment Procedure: A Conceptual Approach. *Tourism Management*, 26 (3), 431-445.

Macarena, L.-O., Blancas, F. J., González, M. & Caballero, R. (2012). Sustainable Tourism Indicators as Planning Tools in Cultural Destinations. *Ecological Indicators*, 18, 659-675.

Manning, E. W. & Dougherty, T. D. (1995). Sustainable Tourism: Preserving the Golden Goose. *Cornell Hotel and Restaurant Administration Quarterly* (April), 29-42.

Mascarenhas, A., Coelho, P., Subtil, E., & Ramos T. B. (2010). The Role of Common Local Indicators in Regional Sustainability Assessment. *Ecological Indicators*, 10, 646-656.

Miller, G. (2001). The Development of Indicators for Sustainable Tourism: Results of a Delphi Survey of Tourism Researchers. *Tourism Management*, 22, 351-362.

Mowforth, M., & Munt, I. (2008). *Tourism Sustainability: Tourism in the World*. London: Routledge.

Rajaonson, J. & Tanguay, G. A. (2012). Strategy for Selecting Sustainable Tourism Indicators for the Gaspésie and Îles de la Madeleine Regions. *Téoros,* Special Issue 2012 (1), 77-84.

Rametsteiner, E., Pülzl, H., Alkan-Olsson, J. & Frederiksen, P. (2010). Sustainability Indicator Development: Science or Political negotiation? *Ecological Indicators,* 11 (1), 61-70.

Reed, M. S., Fraser, E. D. G. & Dougill, A. J. (2006). An Adaptive Learning Process for Developing and Applying Sustainability Indicators with Local Communities. *Ecologicial Economics*, 59, 406-418.

Roberts, S. & Tribe, J. (2008). Sustainability Indicators for Small Tourism Enterprises: An Exploratory Perspective. *Journal of Sustainable Tourism*, 16 (5), 575-594.

Schianetz, K. & Kavanagh, L. (2008). Sustainability Indicators for Tourism Destinations: A Complex Adaptive Systems Approach Using Systemic Indicator Systems. *Journal of Sustainable Tourism*, 16 (6), 601-628.

Sirakaya, E., Jamal, T., & Choi, H. S. (2001). *Developing Tourism Indicators for Destination Sustainability*. In D. B. Weaver (Ed.), Encyclopedia of Ecotourism (pp. 411-432). New York, NY: CAB International.

Stabler, M. (2007). *Tourism Sustainability: The practice*. Wallingford, OX, UK: CAB International.

Tanguay, G. A. & Rajaonson J. (2012). *Indicateurs de tourisme durable. Gaspésie-Îles-de-la-Madeleine*. Gaspésie: Conférence régionale des élus de la Gaspésie-Îles-de-la-Madeleine: Rapport de recherche.

Tanguay, G. A & Rajaonson, J. (2013). Selection and Use of Sustainable Tourism Indicators in the Evaluation of Projects and Policies. *Transfert*, 1, 102-116.

Tanguay, G. A., Rajaonson, J., & Therrien, M. C. (2013). Sustainable Tourism Indicators: Selection Criteria for Policy Implementation and Scientific Recognition. *Journal of Sustainable Tourism*, 21(6), 862-879.

Wahab, S., & Pigram, J. J. J. (2010). *Tourism Growth: Sustainability*. London: Routledge.

Weaver, D. B. (2006). *Sustainable Tourism: Theory and Practice*. London: Routledge.

World Tourism Organization (WTO). (2004). *Indicators of Sustainable Development for Tourism Destinations: A guidebook*. Madrid: UN-WTO.

INDEX

D

S